AF379236

J. Ogden Murray

CONFEDERATE SKETCHES

The Southern Statesman
The Confederate Soldier
The South's Peerless Women

by
Major John Ogden Murray
A Soldier of 1861-1865, C.S.A.

THE CONFEDERATE
REPRINT COMPANY
☆   ☆   ☆   ☆
WWW.CONFEDERATEREPRINT.COM

Confederate Stories
by John Ogden Murray

Originally Published in 1915
under the title Three Stories in One
by Whittet and Shepperson
Richmond, Virginia

Reprint Edition © 2015
The Confederate Reprint Company
Post Office Box 2027
Toccoa, Georgia 30577
www.confederatereprint.com

Cover and Interior Design by
Magnolia Graphic Design
www.magnoliagraphicdesign.com

ISBN-13: 978-0692506523
ISBN-10: 0692506527

DEDICATION

This book is dedicated to the peerless women of the South, whose loyalty, fidelity and devotion to the Confederate Soldier was the inspiration that made him the ideal soldier of the world, and engraved upon the scroll of fame, for herself, a record time cannot efface.

The Author.

CONTENTS

☆　☆　☆　☆

PART I
The Southern Statesman

The Early Years of Jefferson Davis
West Point Academy and Military Service
Davis in the Black Hawk War

Beginning of Davis' Political Career
Service in the Mexican-American War
Davis in the United States Senate

Davis Appointed U.S. Secretary of War
A Base Slander Refuted

Sectional Animosity Intensifies
Historical Background of the Civil War
New England and Slavery
Northern Anti-Negro Prejudice

PART II
The Confederate Soldier

PART III
The South's Peerless Women

PART I
The Southern Statesman

Jefferson Davis

PREFACE

This essay has behind its publication two good and sufficient reasons.

The first reason is to give to the present generation, and our Southern children especially, a truthful idea of Jefferson Davis, President of the Confederate States, and his life's work for the American people, without regard to section, and we hope to refute, so far as we are able to do by this essay, the vile slanders that have been uttered against him and his people by the fanatical pulpit and press of the Northern States.

We want our boys and girls of the South to know their fathers were not Rebels nor Traitors in 1861, but patriots, who obeyed the laws, and loved the Constitution as handed down to us by the men who made it to protect all sections alike. We want the whole world to know Jefferson Davis as we know him, the American Patriot and Statesman.

Second. We want to incite in our children a spirit of study of the causes that led up to the war; we want the world to have a true story of the cruel, unjust and illegal war made upon the South and her people, waged with fanatical malice from 1861 to '65, to take from the States of the South and her people their political liberties granted by the Constitution. We want the world to know the people who hated the law, in their malice, because of the prosperity of the South, and if the conflict was inevitable and had to come, the South in morals had a better reason for her course than did the North.

We want all the world to know that secession did not have its birth in the South in 1861, and we want to show that it was conceived in the brain of a Yankee Statesman and born in the State of Loyal Massachusetts, before Mr. Jefferson Davis was born. We want all the facts presented at the bar of history, and with these facts, when we have passed over the River, our children can refute the charge whenever made that the men who wore the gray and followed Robert E. Lee, were Traitors and Rebels. With this statement, the reasons for this booklet's publication, we present the facts upon which we rest our case.

J. Ogden Murray.

INTRODUCTORY

He who now completes, with attractive words, fitly written, a life size portraiture of Jefferson Davis, will have contributed to his countrymen of the present generation a biography which will teach truth, patriotism and honor by a most notable and noble example. Such a gift to general intelligence has been made after patient research by the author of this volume.

Mr. Davis was the product of worthy, patriotic, Christian ancestry, as well as a result of training throughout his youth and manhood amidst the best associations into the spirit of the citizenship which distinguishes the American Citizen of our Constitutional Government of free States and free Institutions.

His life is itself a book on which the student will eagerly explore a field of great ideas, true ambitions, lofty aspirations, and high endeavors, all of which move together under moral and patriotic restraints to make a character well worthy of a firm place amongst the notably great men of the world.

Mr. Davis, President of the Confederate States, deserves to be understood. He merits honorable treatment. His name and fame are conspicuously connected with the civil and military events of our country's history during the entire period of his long, unsullied, useful life.

Let the lives of all great men from all sections of the Union be fairly and thoroughly considered in the present era of our country's estate, and in view of its greatest opportunity to enlighten the world in the principles and form of that truly good government which all the world seems to be craving now.

Clement A. Evans.

CHAPTER ONE

☆　☆　☆　☆

The Early Years of Jefferson Davis

An epoch in Southern history began June 3rd, 1808. This day Jefferson Davis was born at Fairfield, in the grand old commonwealth of Kentucky, that has given to the South some of its grandest men and peerless women. One hundred years ago this greatest of American patriots was born, destined to be the leader of a liberty loving people whose courage, fidelity to principle, and sacrifices to be made, would write upon the pages of American history a story that would for all time be the admiration of the world. The name of our peerless leader was written upon the scroll of fame by the great Creator from the beginning of time, and He watched over this child, I do believe, blessing him and directing his life's work for the best interests of the grandest people, and purest patriots the world has ever known. I hardly feel able to draw for our children the portraiture of Jefferson Davis, and his life's work for our people; but I shall do the best I can – Angels can do no more.

Jefferson Davis came of revolutionary stock, who helped to carve out with their swords this grand nation, the envy of the world. No American patriot loved his country greater than Jefferson Davis. His childhood days spent in Mississippi were like those of the average American children of his day, spent in going to school, hunting, fishing and such outdoor exercises as were indulged in by our restless boys, who have made the distinguished men of this Republic. His first tuition was in the old log school-house of the earlier days, developing the great mind, forming the noble character that was to make him the peer of any man of his day. He was a child of personal courage, a youth of ability, a man whose strong will and grand intellect made him the leader of men, he idol of our people. When but a child, there was an incident occurred which showed the mettle in his make-up – it is worth reciting.

Jefferson Davis and his sister were constant companions. One day while on their way to school, the boy had been telling his sister never to be afraid, that he was always ready to take care of her and defend her, guard and protect her from harm. Hardly had he finished telling Pollie how brave he would be for her, when a chance to test his courage presented itself. There was a character who lived in the settlement near the Davis farm who very often indulged in the ardent; when in his cups he was inclined to be insolent and ugly. This fellow was a terror to the children of the settlement; they would scamper off at the sight of the old fellow. This day Jefferson and his sister Pollie were on their way to school, passing, as they had to do, to reach the school house, through a thick, heavy woods. The children discovered coming toward them an object they took to be the old drunkard of the settlement, the terror of the children. Pollie became very much alarmed and wanted to run away. Jefferson took her hand and said, "Sister, we will not run; don't be afraid; I will protect you – have no fear." And our young hero boldly advanced to meet the danger. As they approached the object of their fright, instead of meeting the poor old terror of the neighborhood, they came face to face with a magnificent buck, his head high in the air with antlers spread. The children stopped; they had never seen such a beast as this before. The buck came close up, took a good look at the children, turned and scampered off into the forest. When the buck came close to the children the boy put his sister behind him to better protect her and calmly awaited events.

Thus early in childhood we find Jefferson Davis the cool courageous spirit he was during his life, ever ready to defend the weak from the attacks of the strong and oppressor. At the age of seven young Davis was sent by his parents in charge of Major Hinds, a friend of his father, back from Mississippi to Kentucky, and entered as a pupil in a Catholic institute, known as St. Thomas, presided over by the Dominican fathers, who taught the best schools of that day. In those early days there were no steamboats nor railroads. The travel was by stage coach or horseback, and this boy made the long trip passing through the country of the Choctaw and Chickasaw Indians to reach Kentucky. It was on this trip, 1815, Jefferson Davis as a boy first met and formed acquaintance with Gen. Andrew Jackson. The General and his wife treated young Davis with so much kindness that it inspired in the boy's heart a reverence and love for the hero of New Orleans that remained with him during life.

When young Davis arrived at St. Thomas College in Kentucky, he was so frail looking the good priests of the institute took especial care of hm. The Rev. Father Wallace, who became bishop of Nashville, treated young Davis as a son. The reverend father had a bed placed in his own room that the boy might be near him, but Mr. Davis says, Father Wallace never tried to proselyte him from the faith of his father. Young Davis remained at the school for two years when his mother insisted he should return home.

He left Louisville City upon one of the first steamboats put upon the river. On his arrival at home in Mississippi he again took up school work at the county academy. While at this school one of the teachers gave him a task which the boy could not do. He went to the teacher, candidly stated the case, and asked to be relieved. The teacher refused to do this, and insisted that the task should be performed or punishment would follow. The boy, believing himself to be unjustly treated, gathered his books and left the school, going home. He reported his case to his father, candidly giving the details. His father listened attentively to his son, and said, "My son, it is with you to elect whether you will work with your hands or your head. My son cannot be an idler in life. I need cotton pickers and will pay you and give you work."

The boy accepted his father's proffer and went to work. A cotton bag was given him. He went into the field with the hands, and worked day after day in the heat of the burning sun. A few days of this work satisfied young Davis that the school room was much less an evil than cotton picking under the burning sun. He went to his father, stated his inability to work in the field and asked to be allowed to go back to school, which he did, determined to do to the best of his ability the tasks demanded of him. And this determination was the great object of Jefferson Davis' life – to do his duty at all hazard. Duty with him was first.

West Point Academy and Military Service

After a few years at this academy he returned to Kentucky and entered the University at Lexington, from which school he graduated. In 1824 he was appointed a cadet to the military school at West Point. He was then but 17 years of age. His classmates were Albert Sydney Johnson, Leonidas Polk, and others who became famous and wrote their names upon the scroll of heroes in the wars of Mexico and 1861-'65. While at West Point, Cadet Davis was distinguished for his manly, high-toned and lofty character, and his love of justice and truth. To illustrate this phase of his character:

One day one of the professors was lecturing Cadet Davis' class upon the essential qualities necessary to make a soldier. For some unknown reason this professor had formed a great dislike for Cadet Davis. Talking directly to Cadet Davis he said: "I doubt not, sir, there are a great many who in an emergency would become confused and lose their heads, not from cowardice, but from the smallness of their minds." This insult was intended for Cadet Davis who was powerless to resent it, but the cadet bided his time and he had his day. A few days after this, again the same lecturer was teaching the class the process of making fireballs. One of the balls took fire and the room was filled with explosives. Cadet Davis was the first to discover the danger. He very coolly asked the professor: "What shall I do, sir? This fireball is ignited!" The professor said, "Run for your life, sir," and the professor ran for the door, the first to make the exit. Cadet Davis did not flee the danger like the others of his class. He coolly walked over to the burning ball, took it in his hand, raised the window and threw it out upon the grass, and by this presence of mind saved the building and forever silenced his enemy, the professor.

One of the most pronounced features in Mr. Davis' character was his horror of doing the least act that would oppress the weak or wound the feelings of the humblest person. Throughout his whole life he exhibited this strong feature of his character. He was generous, kind, and sincere to his fellowman. He had the true idea of Christian love and charity the Master taught. His heart was filled with love for his fellow-man and devotion to duty. In the year 1828 Cadet Davis graduated from West Point and became a second lieutenant of infantry in the regular army. His first duty was at Fort Crawford now in the State of Wisconsin.

The same characteristic that distinguished him as a cadet made him prominent as an officer and attracted the attention of his superior officers. While stationed at Fort Crawford, Lieut. Davis was detailed in charge of a detachment to cut timber to repair the fort. The lieutenant and his party were in a flatboat going down the stream. They were hailed by a party of Indians who demanded a trade of tobacco. One of the men of the detachment, knowing the ways of the Indians and their treachery, warned Lieut. Davis not to push the boat ashore. "Push the boat further out into the stream," was Lieut. Davis' order. The Indians seeing their prey escaping, yelling with fury, jumped into their canoes and gave chase to Lieut. Davis and his party. The Indians were gaining on the flatboat, the men were greatly excited. Almost exhausted Lieut. Davis, calm and cool bid his men have no fears. He ordered a sail to be made of a blanket, and with this slender chance outsailed his Indian pursuers and saved his detachment from death or a worse fate, Indian captivity. I cite these things to show that Jefferson Davis was a man of thought, a man of resources, a man of courage, who never lost his head.

One other incident on this line before we take up the political life of Mr. Davis. In 1831-32, Col. Morgan, commanding the first infantry, U.S.A., sent Lieut T. R. B. Gardiner to Jordons Ferry, now Duleith, with a small detachment of soldiers to prevent trespassing on the lead mines, west of the Mississippi River. About this time Col. Morgan died and Col. Zachary Taylor took command of the first infantry. The lands upon which the lead mines were located belonged to the Indians who determined to drive out the Whites. Col. Taylor sent Lieuts. Abercombe and Jefferson Davis with a small detachment of men to check the Indians and remove the Whites from the lead mines until such treaties could be made with the Indians to relinquish their ownership in these mines.

These miners, who had taken up claims, were men of determination, and did not intend to remove from the mines without resistance for what they claimed was their right to work the lead. Things about the mines looked rather serious. Lieut. Davis was given charge of the matter of dealing with the miners. He crossed over the river and boldly called the miners together. He informed them of his instructions to remove them from the mines until the Indian title thereto could be obtained by the United States. Among the miners was a redheaded desperado, the leader, who informed Lieut. Davis that the miners had resisted former officers backed by soldiers, and if he, Davis, knew when he was well off he better clear out and take his soldiers with him.

Lieut. Davis said, "I feel sorry for you all, but my orders are to move you by force if I must." He then said to the red-headed desperado and leader, "I want you to walk a few yards into the timber that we may have a private talk." This the fellow consented to do. Lieut Davis candidly explained the Government's reason for the removal of the miners and promised them that all would be protected in their rights when the Government obtained the title for the mines from the Indians. After leaving the desperado Lieutenant Davis walked over to a large group of miners and made his first public speech. At first the miners made ugly remarks, but eventually listened in silence to what Lieut. Davis said. After making his speech he left, telling them to move as he would be compelled to use force if his orders were not obeyed.

Some few weeks after this interview he again crossed the river to talk with the miners. His friends begged him not to go without a force. He took only an orderly and coolly went into a little drinking booth, a resort of the miners. Lieut. Davis bid them all the time of day and said, "My friends, I know you have thought over our last talk and have concluded to accept my terms and are going to drink to my success. So I will treat you all." These rough miners gave him a cheer, and he accomplished by kindness and tact what other men would have used force to do, thus showing himself, although young in years, a born leader of men. For this great success the Iowa legislature passed a vote of thanks many years after, when Col. Davis lay wounded at Saltillo after the battle of Buena Vista.

Davis in the Black Hawk War

Now we shall take up Lieut. Davis in the Black Hawk war and show how he won his spurs, helping to make great the Government that took from him his liberty, his citizenship, and persecuted him as no other American citizen was ever persecuted. When the Black Hawk Indian war began, Gen. Winfield Scott sent two young lieutenants to Dixon, Ill., to accept and muster into the United States service such troops as might present themselves. One of these lieutenants was a man of gentle, fascinating manners, affable, pleasant and courteous, drawing to him those with whom he came in contact. The other lieutenant was just as pleasant but most exceedingly modest. The first was Jefferson Davis, first lieutenant U.S.A., the second Lieut. Anderson, who was in 1861 Maj. Anderson, of Fort Sumter fame. On the morning of the arrival of the first troops for muster, a homely, tall and slender youth presented himself to Lieut. Davis as the captain of the company to be mustered. This homely young man was Abraham Lincoln and the young lieutenant was Jefferson Davis, the man who administered to Abraham Lincoln the first oath of allegiance he ever took to the United States Government. Jefferson Davis became President of the Confederate States, Abraham Lincoln President of the United States, and Lieut. Anderson, a prominent figure in the war of 1861-'65, and thus met for the first time the two men whose names have gone sounding down the corridors of time, names never to be forgotten while time shall last.

In this Indian war Lieut. Davis was brought in close contact with two remarkable men, Col. Boone, son of the famous Daniel Boone, of Kentucky, and Maj. Jesse Bean. The courage and integrity of these two men were beyond question and their implicit faith and confidence in Lieut. Davis was known to the whole army. Maj. Bean was a close observer, he had but little education and was a man of few words. This man took great delight in hearing Lieut. Davis talk, and the lieutenant often talked with Bean about the phenomena of nature, telling him in scientific language the theory of cause and effect. Bean took it all in as Gospel truth, simply because Lieut. Davis said it was true; but one day Bean's faith in Lieut. Davis was almost destroyed or at least badly shaken. Mr. Davis had been explaining to Bean the laws which govern our solar system. Bean listened until Mr. Davis had finished; then turning to him said:

> Lieut. Davis, I have always had great confidence in your learning and great respect for you, and I really did not think you would poke fun at the old man who loves you. As for your story of the earth moving and the stars standing still it is all bosh. Night after night, sir, when watching my beaver traps I have seen the stars rise in the East, sail across the skies and set in the West. No man, not even you, Lieut. Davis, can convince Jesse Bean that the stars stand still.

So Lieut. Davis gave up the scientific education of Bean.

In this Indian war Lieut. Davis proved the mettle of which he was made, fairly and honorably, says his superior officers; he won his spurs and the confidence and love of his men by his coolness, kindness, and courage. At the close of the war, 1832, Lieut. Davis was sent on recruiting service to the city of Louisville. While on this recruiting duty he was called to Lexington. While there the cholera broke out in its most malignant form. The citizens who could, fled from the pest-stricken city. But Lieut. Davis, true to himself, true to his duty, remained at his post looking after the health and comfort of his recruits, regardless of consequences to himself.

An incident while Lieut. Davis was in Lexington again shows his goodness of heart. A poor White man and an old Negro died of cholera. No one cared to risk the burial of these people; not so with Lieut. Jefferson Davis. He found after much difficulty a carpenter and he actually helped him make coffins for these paupers and with the carpenter buried the bodies in the cemetery, even helping to dig the graves. I tell this incident to show the example of the true Christian charity which filled the heart of Jefferson Davis, and I tell you this was the prominent feature in his character during his whole life – duty and love to his fellowman. How base is the slander, how malignant the hate, how vile the tongues of those who charge Mr. Davis with cruelty. How could such a heart as beat in the breast of our beloved chief harbor one cruel thought against a fellowman.

CHAPTER TWO

Beginning of Davis' Political Career

In 1835 Mr. Davis resigned from the army, retiring to private life. In 1843 he began his political career. In a canvass as elector at large for Polk and Dallas from Mississippi in 1845 Mr. Davis was elected to Congress. But prior to his election to Congress he was defeated for the legislature of Mississippi. In these pages we can give but brief sketches of this great American patriot. But I hope to paint a portraiture that will give an insight into the greatness of this man, Jefferson Davis. Before he was a candidate for the State legislature and subsequently elected to Congress he was never a candidate before the people for any position. At the time Mr. Davis was a candidate for the legislature what was then known as the act of repudiation was foremost of all questions in the minds of the people of Mississippi. It was paramount to all other questions. Mr. Davis' position on this question was simply this: He held that the Union Bank Bonds did not constitute a debt of the State and the debt as claimed by those who opposed him was unconstitutional; that the question was one the courts should determine. If the court held the debt legal and right then it should be paid, but if the debt, as he claimed, was unconstitutional, then the State should not pay it, and upon this issue he was defeated for the legislature; and upon this flimsy testimony the charge that Mr. Davis was a repudiationist is based. During the Civil War the United States Government went as to send Robert J. Walker, its financial agent, all over Europe, to promulgate this slander against Mr. Davis. Why Mr. Walker, who was personally familiar with all the facts in the case and fully understood Mr. Davis' position, could loan himself to this scheme of slander is to say the least strange. There can be no excuse for his conduct. He was a senator from Mississippi and could not help but know Mr. Davis' position on this question.

In 1844 Mr. Davis loomed up a star upon the political sky, as a party leader. In the national convention held this year Mr. Davis was a delegate. Van Buren was the choice of a large portion of the Democratic party. In the Mississippi State convention a resolution was offered that the delegates from Mississippi should be instructed to vote for Van Buren as long as there was a reasonable chance for his nomination by the convention. Mr. Davis amended this resolution by making John C. Calhoun second choice of the State of Mississippi, which motion was passed, and now Mr. Davis was before the people a party leader, which position he never lost. On December 8, 1845, Mr. Davis took his seat in Congress as a representative from the State of Mississippi. On the 29th of December he offered his resolution which was: That the Committee on Military Affairs be instructed to inquire into the expediency of converting some of the forts owned by the United States into military schools of instruction. His next resolution was to establish a post route direct and daily between Montgomery, Ala., and Jackson, Miss.

His first speech in Congress was made Feb. 6, 1846; the Oregon Question was before the House. From this speech I will quote such portions as will show the force and power of this great man and show how he detested hypocrisy and cant. This hatred for anything insincere never modified during his life. In this speech he said:

> The opinion has gone out that no politician dare to be the advocate of peace. When war is mooted, that will be an evil hour. The sands of our republic will be nearly run when it shall be in the power of any demagogue or fanatic to raise a war clamor and control the legislature of the country. Evils of war must fall upon the people and with them war feeling should originate. We, their representatives, are but the mirror to reflect the light and never should become the torch to fire the pile. We, sirs, cannot expect, we should not require our adversary to submit to more than we would bear, and I ask after the notice has been given and the twelve months have expired, who would allow Great Britain to exercise exclusive jurisdiction over Oregon? If we resist such an act by force of arms before our-

selves perform it we should prepare for war.

He then drew a comparison between the annexation of Texas and Oregon occupation, denying the South had been inconsistent in treating this Oregon question. He asked:

Who are the men who impute for us of the South sordid motives? They are the same men who resisted Texan annexation and most eagerly press on the immediate occupation of Oregon. The source is worthy the suspicion. There are the men whose constitutional scruples resisted a country gratuitously offered to us, but now they look forward to gaining Canada by conquest. In event of war with England I pledge the loyalty of Mississippi. Do you pledge your States?

How fortunate for the country that Congress had one man who dared do right and defend from the aspersions and slanders of the Northern fanatics the people of the South. This debate brought out very clearly another characteristic of Mr. Davis. His love for those memories that formed the glory of all the States. He said:

In the service of my country I know no North nor South nor East nor West from sire to son. If envy is eating the bonds with which our fathers expected to bind us forever, the cause does not come from the South; our Southern atmosphere does not furnish the cause to divide the country. When ignorance led by fanatical hate armed by all unchangeableness assails the domestic institution of the South I try to forgive for the sake of the righteous among the wicked. I leave to silent contempt the malign prediction of the member from Ohio and remember the manly sentiments of the gentlemen from the West.

Closing his speech, Mr. Davis uttered these prophetic words:

The grants of power are general and therefore many things must attach as incident. If the States deny the means necessary to the existence of the Government nothing is more sure than it will usurp them and a conflict will arise between rival powers injurious to both. If, on the other hand, the Federal Government by indirection seeks more than is proper to its functions and necessary to their exercise, indiscriminate opposition may be general and liberality of patriotism be lost in the conflict. The perpetuity of our union requires the States, whenever the grants of the Constitution are inadequate to the purpose for which it was ordained, to add them from their sovereignty as they may be needed.

How far this great man's prophetic eye looked into the future and saw the disaster that was to follow the fanaticism of the North and her hatred for the South and her people. Mr. Davis loved the Union with a patriot's devotion. He loved the Constitution made by our fathers for all sections of our country, and he never ceased to plead that it should not be destroyed by the fanatics of the North.

Service in the Mexican-American War

In 1845 the Texas annexation took place. Mexico threatened to invade Texas. Gen. Taylor with the United States army was ordered to protect the Texas border The war cloud hung over the country. President Polk offered the appointment of brigadier-general of volunteers to Mr. Davis. He declined. Read why he did so: "I prefer to be elected by the volunteer troops I command. After the election and the elective right of the volunteers ceases, the appointing power should be the governors of the States whose troops are to be commanded by the general."

So great was Mr. Davis' love and respect for the rights of each State and his fellowman no honors could tempt him to overstep the line marked by equity and justice. Before Mr. Davis left Washington for the scene of war he called upon Gen. Winfield Scott to say farewell. The general tried to persuade Mr. Davis to arm but four companies of his regiment with rifles. Mr Davis insisted his regiment should all have rifles; that with rifles the Mississippians would fight better with this arm as they were used to handling it. They had no faith in the old flint-lock arms used by the Government. He showed his fine judgment in this matter, insisted and obtained rifles, and his proof of the fact that he knew what arm was best for his men was proven on many a bloody battlefield in Mexico, when the Mississippi troops under command of Jefferson Davis showed their perfect use of the Mississippi rifle as did their descendants in 1861-'65. Gen. John E. Wool said, in special orders, this of Col. Davis and his regiment: "The Mississippi Riflemen, under Col. Davis, were highly conspicuous for gallantry and steadiness at Monterey, acting like veteran troops. Col. Davis, though severely wounded, remained in the saddle until the close of the battle; his distinguished coolness and courage and heavy loss of his regiment on this day entitles him to the particular notice of the Government." This report was made by Gen. Wool in Mexico, in 1849.

Davis in the United States Senate

After the Mexican war was over Mr. Davis returned to his home in Mississippi, fully determined to settle down in private life. But the people of Mississippi had other views and needed Mr. Davis' services in the United States Senate. Gov. A. G. Brown appointed Mr. Davis United States Senator for Mississippi, just two months after Mr. Davis returned from Mexico. There was one general approval throughout the State when Gov. Brown made the appointment. When Mr. Davis took his seat in the United States Senate he was suffering much with his wound and compelled to use crutches. The members of the Senate gave the young Mississippian a cordial and unreserved welcome as a member of the 29th Congress. Mr. Davis had won reputation as a brilliant young member, as a soldier over the border he had won his spurs in defense of his country's honor.

He, with his regiment, had demonstrated American valor on the battlefield and won the love of his fellow countrymen. Mr. Davis was appointed in the Senate on several important committees, the most important being that of Military Affairs. Early in January there arose in the Senate a debate which gave proof to the country of Mr. Davis' intelligent conception of all questions connected with Mexico. Mr. Cass, of Michigan, had reported from the Military Committee what was called the "Ten Regiment Bill." This bill was inspired by the War Department. Mr. Calhoun, of South Carolina, opposed this bill as he had opposed the Mexican War – in fact, all the Southern Senators opposed this bill. Mr. Calhoun saw in the bill the specter of a conquered country, a suspended autonomy. While Mr. Crittenden could see nothing in the bill but the great bugbear of a military Frankenstein to destroy all that was good, not so with Mr. Davis. In answer to the objections of Messrs. Calhoun, Crittenden, and others to this bill he took a broad, intelligent view of the situation. In answer to the fears of these gentlemen that Mexico would ultimately be absorbed by the United States and present to the world another dismembered Poland, Mr. Davis said:

> I can accept Mr. Calhoun's resolution and still vote for this bill. Let me ask you, gentlemen, Is Mexico conquered? Is any part of it conquered? Conquest, as laid down by some writers, is three kinds. Ruin is one of these kinds of conquest, but we have not ruined Mexico and God forbid we ever

should. The moral feeling of this country would never justify such a course. Another mode of conquest is to hold a country by controlling its government; that is not suited to the genius of our country. We send no pro-consul abroad – no provincial army to direct the government of the country. We recognize as the great basis of all institutions self-government. The other mode of conquest is by colonizing a country. We cannot do that. In neither of these modes, then, have we conquered Mexico.

To Mr. Crittenden's dread of the regular soldier, Mr. Davis said:

If this country were invaded I would turn, sir, to the great body of the militia. I use the terms of volunteer and militia as synonymous – for its defense. But when we are engaged in a foreign war and only defensive operations are carried on, we then have reached the point where regulars are the force, which should be employed where the militia may not be called upon to justify the disruption of society which would result if we brought out that grand class of soldiers who constitute our volunteers. As long as you keep the high-bred men for battle they will bear any privation, submit to every restraint, and discharge every duty. But you cannot expect these men who have broken all home ties in order to fight for their country, will sacrifice themselves to the mere duty of the sentinel.

How well proven was this declaration of Mr. Davis shown in 1861-'65? The Confederate army was an army of high-bred men and they were the ideal soldiers of the world. In the course of the debate upon this "Ten Regiment Bill" it was made clear that he was just the man for chairmanship of the Senate Military Committee, and to this position he was elected in the 31st Congress almost unanimously. Thirty-two votes were given him to five votes for all others. On July 6, President Polk laid before the Senate a copy of the treaty of peace between the United States and Mexico.

While in the U.S. Senate Mr. Davis took care to put himself on record at all times against the centralization of power by the general government. On one occasion, he said:

> I hold this whole system of internal improvements by the Federal Government is an assumption of power not conferred by the Constitution, but in this case I approve this appropriation for the repair of this dam in the Ohio River for the sole reason the Government has constructed it, but I, while voting for this bill, do not surrender my idea of the literal translation of the Constitution.

The power to prescribe rules for commerce among the States was surrendered to the Government and thereby the States were deprived of the power to impose restrictions or levy duty upon the commerce of each other. To regulate is to make rules not to provide means. On April 20, 1848, Mr. Hall of New Hampshire, hurled a firebrand into the Senate. The bill was in relation to riots and unlawful assemblies in the District of Columbia. The avowed purpose of this bill was to punish an assemblage of armed citizens of the District who had made an attack upon an Abolitionist paper, *The National Era*, published in Washington, which had been making attacks on the citizens and Southern members of Congress. This bill was cunningly drawn. It said not a word about an attempt which had stirred the capitol but a few days before, when the Schooner Pearl, manned by a band of non-resident men, attempted stealing seventy-odd Negroes belonging under the Constitution to citizens of the District. Mr. Davis said:

> Your bill speaks loudly for one class of property, that in a newspaper, but it is dumb as a mute upon that to be accorded to another kind of property guaranteed by the Constitution. The time has come for Congress to interpose the legislation necessary to punish the men who come within our jurisdiction, acting in fact in morals as incendiaries, coming right here within the limits of the jurisdiction of Congress to steal property recognized by the Constitution. Is this district to be made the field of abolition struggle? Is this Senate chamber to be made the hot bed of sedition and treason? Why is it that these fanatics will introduce these insults to the South?

Turning to Hall, he said:

> Sir, if civil discord is to be thrown from this chamber upon the land, if the fire is to be kindled herewith which is to burn the temple of our Union, if it is to be made the center from which civil war is to radiate, let the conflict begin. I am ready for one

to meet any incendiary who, dead to every feeling of patriotism, attempts to introduce it.

They were strong words from Mr. Davis for he was always inclined to discountenance more than to urge disunion as a remedy for the dissensions within the Union. He loved the Union. He loved the Constitution. He stood for the law and obedience to the law. He had no sympathy nor patience with the fanatical disruptors of the Union of the North whom he knew would sooner or later destroy the law and the guarantees of the Constitution. Later on came up the bill to admit Oregon. Here, again, Mr. Davis showed himself a master of statesmanship. This was one of his greatest speeches, made July 12, 1847, in the 30th Congress. He said:

Congress had no power to change the conditions or to strip the master of his property, entering a territory with his property. The South does not ask for the introduction of slavery into Oregon, but it does demand protection for its property. On the acquisition of territory the condition of slavery is not changed. The Government acquired no new power over it, but stood merely in the position of an agent for its protection. Until a territory becomes a State the law must remain inviolable until abrogated by the State enactments.

Further on in this same speech, Mr. Davis said: "The slave must be made fit for freedom by education and discipline and thus made unfit for slavery." He showed that all disorder that existed in the

South was not of domestic origin, but came from New England and Great Britain and imposed upon the South the strongest obligation to rise in self-defense. He spoke of the fraternal feeling which induced the South to make common cause of war with the North against England. The South had no cause of complaint; it was flourishing by its trade with Great Britain. But the South's great love for our common country and the fraternal feeling for the people of the North and principle made us take up arms against Great Britain, and in return for this the North paid us in treachery, deceit, and a demand that we change our domestic institutions to gratify the selfishness of the fanatics. Mr. Davis said:

> The South does not ask any special privileges, but we do demand there shall be no interference with our legal rights given us by the Constitution. You, of the North, resent such interference; why should you ask us of the South to tolerate the open violation of the Constitution, you inject or try to do so into every bill you present to the Senate? You denounce our institutions and our people. Are we, sirs, not as good and loyal citizens as you are? Have riots, conflagrations, and destruction of private property been more frequent in the South than in the non-slave holding States? If slavery be a sin, you are guilty, for by you came its introduction. As owners of the commercial marine you imported these slaves, you sold them in the South, and you are parties to the contract that made them legal property. If you repent of this, show your repentance by keeping the moral obligations you made

when you sold to the South her slaves. You forget in your fanaticism that the Government is the agent of the States; it is simply the creature of the States from which it derives all its power. Let those who possess opportunity to judge the men who have grown up in the presence of slavery as it exists in the United States and say if they are not useful, noble citizens. Compare the slaves of the South with the free Blacks of the North and tell me which is the most contented and happy? One suffers all the pain of physical want; they fill penitentiaries and pauper institutes. View the slave of the South. He is moral, honest and well cared for.

This speech was one of the many powerful defenses he made on the floor of the Senate for his beloved South and her people.

In the spring of 1848, Gen. Lopez called one evening to see Senator Davis at his Washington home and invited Mr. Davis to take charge and command of an expedition to free Cuba, liberate her from the Spanish bonds that held her. There was to be $100,000 given Mr. Davis when he took charge of the affair and $100,000 and a coffee plantation when the Island should be free. In telling this to friends, Mr. Davis said: "If it had been consistent with my idea of duty I would have accepted." This same offer was made to General, then Major, Robert E. Lee. but he, too, did not think it consistent to accept after he had advised with Mr. Davis.

CHAPTER THREE

Davis Appointed U.S. Secretary of War

Mr. Davis served in the Senate in the 31st Congress, 1849-50. It was in this Congress that Mr. Clay presented his famous compromise resolution. This was a Congress of giants. Among this great aggregation were men whose names will never fade from the pages of American history. Davis, Calhoun, Clay, Badger, N.C; Butler, S.C; Hunter, of Virginia, from the South. Webster, Seward, Hamlin, of the North; Benton, Corwin, Douglas, of the West. In this Congress came the first blow struck at the Union. The anti-slavery movement spread so rapidly that it became aggressive and arrogant. During the debate on this resolution of Mr. Clay, Mr. Seward, of New York, attempted to introduce a resolution, that the Rev. Father Mathew, a great temperance orator of that day, should be invited to a seat within the bar of the Senate Mr. Clemens objected to the reverend gentleman being invited inside of the Senate bar, because he had denounced the South as little better than a band of pirates. To this objection Mr. Seward spoke and urged his resolution be adopted. In reply Mr. Davis tore off Mr. Seward's mask of insincerity and laid bare before the world his hypocrisy and the cant of the North. "The Union, without the Constitution, we hold to be a curse; with the Constitution we hold it a blessing and will never abandon it." In this speech he warned and begged the fanatics of the North to abandon their work of destroying the Union. He said: "The people of the South know their rights. This generation all maintain the character of their fathers. They will sustain the institutions they inherited if necessary by war. They will march up to meet the issue face to face. Do not, I plead, make this necessary."

In this session of the 31st Congress the real agitation of the abolition party began. Vermont, Massachusetts, New Hampshire and Pennsylvania all sent petitions to Congress on the question of slavery. A reference to the *Congressional Record* will show that Mr. Davis was always in his seat, always on the alert to protect the South from the slanders and hate of the fanatics who were bent on destroying the Union, to build it up again upon a basis of unconstitutional principles and foundation of Negro equality which they succeeded in doing after years of agitation, slander and misrepresentation of the South.

In this year, 1849, there was a great political campaign in State politics of Mississippi. Mr. Davis had just been elected a Senator for six years. His high sense of honor prevented him from taking part in this campaign. The success of the Democratic party would be endangered by the nomination of Gen. Quitman who held to the Calhoun doctrine of nullification. The party turned to Mr. Davis, his name was announced for Governor and he at once resigned his seat in the U.S. Senate to enter the State campaign. Mr. Davis had just six weeks in which to work. He was broken in health and could not bear the fatigue of campaigning. He was defeated and now determined to retire from public life and enter again upon the private life of a planter. He had just begun to feel again the comfort of home life at Briarfield when Mr. Franklin Pierce (1852) was elected President. He wrote, urging Mr. Davis to enter his cabinet, pleading with him to come to Washington if only for the inauguration. When Mr. Davis arrived in Washington the 4th of March, 1853, Mr. Pierce brought all the pressure he could to bear upon Mr. Davis to induce him to take the portfolio of the War Department. Mr. Davis yielded.

December 7, 1853, as Secretary of War, he submitted his first report. Like all his public documents it was marked by a dignity of style which invested dead facts with life, but added force and argument to his work. While in President Pierce's cabinet Mr. Davis was the conspicuous figure, making such vast improvements in the work of that department that even those opposed to Mr. Pierce's administration were compelled to give praise to the Secretary of War. Take, today, the opinion of every old officer of the United States Army, and he will without hesitation tell you that Jefferson Davis was the best as he was the greatest Secretary of War who ever held that portfolio.

He established new army posts west of the Mississippi River for the protection of emigration. He put a strong post at El Paso. He made the raids of the terrible Comanche Indians across the border more hazardous for them and thereby diminished their depredations. He took up and corrected and perfected the recruiting service. His influence for good diminished the desertions from the army. He recommended an increase of pay for the private soldier and promotion for the non-commissioned officers to that of commissioned officers. His great sense of equity and justice dictated this reform. He insisted that only intelligent men of character should be enlisted, thus fixing a higher standard in the ranks of the army. He urged the defense of our coasts, and he it was that took practical steps to have the most practicable and economical route for a railroad from the Mississippi River to the Pacific Ocean, and to him alone is this first inception of a railroad due.

A Base Slander Refuted

It was Jefferson Davis as Secretary of War who declared the Government should undertake nothing private enterprise could accomplish. He gave his views for this opinion and they have never been controverted. He urged the establishment of an armory on Western waters and the removal of one of the armories from the East to the West. Let me say here this one act alone disposes of that base, malicious slander that he, when in office, strengthened the South in its military work at the expense of the North. Under the supervision of the War Department, Secretary of War, Davis energetically prosecuted the extension of the capital. Under his supervision the grand waterway for supplying Washington City with drinking water was built. A splendid stone aqueduct stands but a few miles from Washington, a monument to his earnest labor. The engineer, Capt. C. M. Meigs, who had charge of the great work under Mr. Davis, had the impudence in his bigotry and zeal to have Mr. Davis' name erased from the tablet on the bridge, but by the efforts of Mrs. Cornelia Brach Stone, President General of the U. D. C, the name of Mr. Davis has been restored to Cabin John Bridge.

Mr. Davis' second report as Secretary of War is an interesting document. I commend it to all military students. Report of Secretary of War, second session, thirty-third Congress, Executive Document. No. 1, 1854. The city of Dubuque today is indebted to Mr. Davis for her grand ice harbor the best on the river from St. Paul's to New Orleans. In the third report of Mr. Davis as Secretary of War we find many more improvements made by him. He stopped the making of smoothbore arms and had improved rifles – breechloading and other patterns made. Those which were valueless to the soldier as a defense, were cast aside and better things substituted. In his fourth report all the Indian troubles on the plains had ended or nearly so. Mr. Davis was a civil-service reformer. He knew no politics when he was making appointments for office. Fitness alone not politics was his rule. Neither Whig nor Democrat could hold office if he could not fill the position up to the standard set by Mr. Davis. He had the system of tactics revised and sent Capt. Hardee to France to study the best modes. He organized and perfected the army signal corps. On one occasion a man who knew nothing about large guns, their expansion and contraction under heat, went to Mr. Davis to endorse his invention. After the Secretary of War had talked to the inventor and found out his total ignorance he refused to endorse the invention. The inventor took his gun to Congress, asked and got an appropriation to have his gun made and tested. The inventor made requisition on the War Department for assistance which was accorded him. When the gun was finished he applied for a gunner to fire it, but to this Mr. Davis said, "Sir, I cannot give you a man's life and you must find some one else to fire your gun. I will not order an officer of the U. S Army to do it." As the inventor did not care to risk his own life the gun was never fired.

John W. Forney, of Philadelphia, said of Mr. Davis in his paper:

Jefferson Davis was blessed with many accomplishments. He was statesman and alike a soldier. He was as conversant with the smallest minutiæ of his department. He devoted himself to the decoration of the Capitol. He stood by Capt. C.

M. Meigs in all his work, Jefferson Davis was the greatest Secretary of War we ever had and the best friend to worthy young men I ever knew.

On March 4, 1857, Mr. Davis resigned his office as Secretary of War. The parting between President Pierce and his Secretary of War was tender and sincere. Mr. Buchanan had been elected to succeed Mr. Pierce as president.

CHAPTER FOUR

Sectional Animosity Intensifies

Now came those horrible days of 1850 to 1861. Mr. Davis was again in the United States Senate. John Brown, that prince of scoundrels and murderers, a fanatic of fanatics, had gathered together a band of lawless characters and invaded the State of Virginia. On the night of October 16, 1859, this band of cut throats virtually began the war of 1861-'65, bringing the results that Mr. Davis time and time again spoke of and deprecated. John Brown's first victim was an inoffensive Colored man named Stephens who refused to join Brown and his band of murderers. In the excited condition of the public mind in the South this raid of Brown's into the State of Virginia made the condition acute. Volunteers rushed to the scene. Brown and part of his party were captured, tried and hung for their treason and murder. Fowler, in his work, *Sectional Controversy*, says in cities and towns in the North on the day John Brown was hung at Charlestown, Va., bells were tolled and prayers offered in the churches. He was honored as a saint and martyr, when in truth he was but a cowardly murderer of women and children. Men of his own party associates have so denounced him. Be what he may, he was a violator of the laws of the State of Virginia, and that grand old Commonwealth hung him as she would any other criminal. It was proven that both members of the Senate and House of Congress had contributed money to further Brown's scheme to add fuel to the flame.

Hinton Helper, of North Carolina, wrote that infamous book, *The Impending Crisis*. The book intensified the feeling between the North and the South. The proposition of his book was to abolish slavery in the South by first inciting a revolution among that class called "poor Whites." This book also urged that there should be no fellowship in religion, no charity for slave-owners. Murder and rapine was the religion of this fanatic. Congress opened December 7, 1859. Incredible as it may seem this Helper book was purchased by Northern Senators and the fanatics of the North and sent out as campaign matter. It was scattered over the South by the secret agents of the abolitionist societies of the North. Northern members of the Senate openly ignored the decisions of the Supreme Court and declared their intention to violate the rights of property within the territories guaranteed by the Constitution.

The abolitionist took cause with Stephen A. Douglas. The whole country was in uproar. Conservative Northern Democrats and Southern Democrats stood together to stem this tide that they saw must dash the ship of Union to pieces upon the rocks of fanaticism. About this moment when lines were drawn tight such sentiments were heard from leaders all over the North, that the most hopeful men of that day felt the hour had come and the death knell of the Union struck.

Historical Background of the Civil War

Now we will take up the crisis that culminated in the war of 1861-'65 and as introductory want to call attention to some facts that led up to the war. There is a tendency, a disposition by some in the South to forget the past, to treat the history of the past as a closed book, and teach our children to let the book forever remain closed. This would be gladly done by every man in the South who honestly wore the gray, if it did not present us to the world as accepting the explanations of the fanatics of the North as the true causes of the war, and the unfriendliness of the sections against our people and our domestic laws and institutions.

We will designate the people of the two sections, North and South; one we will call Puritans, the other Cavaliers. Hume, the English historian, and McCauley, with other European writers, say: "The Puritans of England, up to the date of the Stuarts, looked upon all who did not agree with them as Amalekites, idolaters, whom they, the Puritans, as God's only chosen people, were ordained and commissioned to punish and bring into the Puritan fold," and it was this stock, says C. B. Taylor, in his *History of the United States*, that came over in the *Mayflower* (their ark) and brought with them their commissions to burn witches, burn the tongues of Quakers and do other things in God's holy name, like dictating morals and manners to the people of the South.

The Southerners were immigrants from England, Scotland, France and all Europe, without special commissions from the Lord to teach their fellowman how to worship. The people who settled in the South, in religion were Protestants, Catholics, Jews, who tolerated each other as men and brothers. They had divorced Church and State, giving each man the right to worship God as he believed.

We admit for argument's sake that the Puritan or New Englander was God's chosen people and New England his inheritance. When we come to read the history of these people at this day we cannot but view with horror the atrocities perpetrated upon the Narragansett Indians in 1675, and question if God's own people would commit such acts. When we read in Irving's *History of New York*, how the cute men of New England counterfeited the local currency of the Dutch, cheating them out of their gold, herrings and cheese, this makes us again question if these early Puritan pilgrims were God's chosen people.

Now, for a few notes from early history to show the attitude of the two sections, which will enable the student to hunt up the full details. Of the incident of the tea tax which brought on the struggle between the English crown and the colonies, Senator Geo. F. Hoar says: "The Southern colonies had not the slightest particle of personal interest." See Montgomery's *U.S. History*. Shortly after the Declaration of Independence there was a formal move made to form a compact of States. When the draft of a constitution was under discussion, Rutledge, of South Carolina, objected to its provisions. Why? Because he doubted the good faith of those chosen people of God who even this early were trying to make the Southern colonies subject to the whims and dictation of the Eastern colonies. Some incidents in the time when Washington was given command of the Colonial army: In November, 1775, after Washington had been some months in command of the New England troops at Boston, he wrote: "Such a mercenary spirit pervades the whole that I should not be surprised at any disaster that may happen. * * * Could I have foreseen what I have experienced and am likely to experience, no consideration upon earth would have induced me to accept this command."

Historian Benjamin Franklin Grady wrote:

In December, 1775, John Adams, a member of the Marine Committee in the Continental Congress, opposed the appointment of John Paul Jones to a captaincy in the navy, whose election Joseph Hewes was advocating. Afterwards Hewes wrote: "The attitude of Mr. Adams was in keeping with the always imperious and often arrogant tone of the Massachusetts people at that time." * * * *

In November, 1776, the British brigantine

Active, loaded with clothing for Gen. Burgoyne's army, was captured off the coast of Cape Breton by the *Alfred*, commanded by Capt. John Paul Jones. He appointed "Lieutenant Spooner" to take command of the prize, to proceed with all haste to Edenton, North Carolina, and deliver her to "Robert Smith, Esquire," who was the partner of Joseph Hewes, through whose influence, being a member of the Marine Committee in the Continental Congress, Jones had been appointed Senior First Lieutenant in the navy. But "Lieutenant Spooner" carried the prize to Dartmouth, Massachusetts, and delivered it to his brother who was prize agent. * * * *

When John Paul Jones, commanding the *Ranger*, was in St George's Channel planning a descent on the Irish coast by night in order to surprise and capture the *Drake*, a twenty-gun British ship, his New England officers would not consent to the movement. Jones says in his *Narrative*: "This project, however, greatly alarmed my lieutenants; they were poor, they said, and their object was gain, not honor; they accordingly excited disobedience among the ship's company, by persuading them that they had a right to determine whether the measures adopted by me were well concerted or not." * * * *

In 1787 the Congress of the Confederation, eight States represented, sold to a number of Northern gentlemen (including Dr. Manasseh Cutler, Gen. Rufus Putnam, Gen. S.H. Parsons and Col. William Duer) 5,000,000 acres of land in Ohio, and accepted for payment $3,500,000 of "Continental money," which was then worth one-eighth of its face value. In other words, these gentlemen purchased a tract of land as large as the State of New Jersey at less than nine cents per acre, thus laying the foundations for the "expansion" of New England in the lands which Virginia had ceded for the common benefit of all the States. * * * *

During the war of 1812 John Lowell published in Boston a paper which he called "The Road to Ruin," in which (as quoted by Carey in his *Olive Branch*) he thus spoke of the trading class of the people: "They engage in lawless speculations, sneer at restraints of conscience, laugh at perjury, mock at legal restraints, and acquire an ill-gotten wealth at the expense of public morals," &c., thus manifesting a disposition which, in the estimation of some people, has not entirely disappeared yet, as we may infer from this remark of Senator Bradley, of Kentucky, in a speech he delivered in the Senate on the 4th of May, 1909: "Mr. President," he said, "one more word and I am through. Give to Kentucky fair protection of her interests" – the right, he meant, to "prosper" at the expense of other States – "and I guarantee you it will be but a short time until Kentucky is as certainly a Republican State as the great State of Massachusetts."

All these quotations from early history give an idea of what the people of the South had to deal with in 1861-'65, and their commercialism always with them above principle. Now a few more quotations:

While the people of New England were fretting about the non-intercourse acts of Jefferson's Administration, "Algernon Sidney" (probably

J.Q. Adams) addressed "An Appeal" to them (see *State Papers*, 2nd Sess., 10th Cong.) in which this question appears: "Recur to the period between peace and the present Government. Did not the commercial States enrich themselves at the expense of the agricultural?" * * * *

Referring to this same period and particularly to the disappearance of the wealthy men of Colonial times, Hildreth says in his *History of the United States*: "In their place a new moneyed class has sprung up, especially in the Eastern States, men who had grown rich in the course of the war as sutlers, by privateering, by speculations in the fluctuating paper money, and by other operations not always of the most honorable kind." Vol. III., p. 465. * * * *

In 1790, while Congress was planning a new tariff bill, Massachusetts sent a petition asking "a remission of duties on all the dutiable articles used in the fisheries," whether re-exported or not – salt, rum, tea, sugar, molasses, iron, coarse woolens, lines and hooks, sailcloth, cordage and tonnage, "and also premiums and bounties." And this petition asked for all these special favors for a people to whom John Jay thus referred to in the *Federalist* about two years before this: "With France and with Britain we are rivals in the fisheries, and can supply their markets cheaper than they can themselves, notwithstanding any efforts to prevent it by bounties on their own or duties on foreign fish."

Now we will take up facts closer to 1861-'65.

As a result of sectional privileges and incidental favors enjoyed by the North from the beginning of the Union, Kettell calculates that the annual flow of money from the South to the North at the time he wrote (1860) amounted to $231,500,000, and the hope that the South could ever free herself from her vassalage had utterly vanished, since at that time the Senate of the United States was composed of thirty Southern and thirty-six Northern members, and some of the territories were about ready to come in and strengthen the North.

To all this evidence it is hardly necessary to add that no Northerner has ever charged that any Southern statesman ever asked for the passage of a law to enable any Southern man, corporation or State to "prosper" at the expense of the Northern States. Nor can there be any doubt of the truth of the statement in *The Origin of the Late War*, a work written by George Lunt, a Massachusetts lawyer. He says: "Of four several compromises between the two sections since the Revolutionary War, each has been kept by the South and violated by the North."

This is the evidence given by a Northern man (Lunt) who had no interest in the South.

New England and Slavery

1. In 1638 – eighteen years after that noted Jamestown incident – the Salem slave-ship, the *Desire*, brought into Massachusetts a number of Negroes, and found ready sale for them. This, says Moore (*Notes*, &c.) "was not a private individual speculation; it was the enterprise of the authorities of

the Colony." But in one volume of the *American History Stories*, published by the Educational Publishing Company, of Boston, it is said that the Georgians introduced slavery into their Colony because they "were not a God-fearing people as were the Puritans and Quakers." And this book has found its way into Southern schools!

2. In 1641 Massachusetts adopted her "body of liberties" as a written Constitution of Government, in which this provision occurs: "There shall never be any bond slavery, villainage or captivity amongst us, unless it be lawful captives taken in just wars and such strangers as willingly sell themselves or are sold to us" – many Indians "willingly" accepting slavery in preference to death when permitted to choose.

3. In 1643 Massachusetts Bay, Plymouth, Connecticut and New Haven formed a Confederation, mutually agreeing, among other stipulations, to surrender fugitive slaves.

4. In 1676 the New Englanders exterminated the Indian tribe which under Massasoit had befriended them for half a century, killing six hundred men and one thousand women and children in one battle and selling the few survivors as slaves, among these being the nine-year-old grandson of Massasoit. He was shipped to Bermuda; and this was done after Rev. Samuel Arnold, of Marshfield, and Rev. John Cotton, of Plymouth, had advised that he be "butchered."

5. In 1768, according to a British report (see

Kettell) 6,700 Negroes were shipped by Northern slavers from the west coast of Africa; and, if we adopt the Jamaica price, these traders carried home more than one million of dollars.

6. In October, 1905, according to the *New York Evening Post*, an insurance policy was shown to a gentleman in that city which was issued to a New England Company, "about 1860," on a cargo of slaves.

7. The slave trade was one of the most gainful employments of New England ships up to 1861. In that year the *Nightingale*, commanded by Francis Bowen, of Boston, was captured on the African coast, having on board 961 Negroes, and was "expecting more," and while she was being captured nine other slaves escaped. Naval War Records, Vol. I.

Slavery being unprofitable in Massachusetts, it was a common practice to give away Negro children "like puppy dogs." I do not suppose this can be denied by any fanatic for its history.

Northern Anti-Negro Prejudice

Adopting the rate of increase of the Colored population of this country from 1880 to 1890 as the normal rate, per decade, I find that after the courts of Massachusetts began to decide that the children of slaves were free at their birth, the Colored population of that State, between 1800 and 1830, fell 2,386 below what it should have been. What became of these unfortunate beings we may never know; but possibly the legislature of North Carolina had them in mind when, in 1786, it enacted that any person who brought a slave into this State from a State which had made provision for the liberation of its slaves, "should enter into a bond with sufficient surety in the sum of fifty pounds" for the removal of the slave back to the State he brought him, and that if he failed to comply with the requirement of the bond he should be liable to a fine of one hundred dollars.

In 1788 Massachusetts adopted a regulation that Negroes from other States, bond or free, could not settle in her borders unless they carried with them certificates of citizenship, and that a violator of the law should be flogged if he refused to leave the State after being warned by a justice of the peace.

One of the first laws adopted by the State of Ohio, which had been settled chiefly by New Englanders, was that no Colored person from another State should migrate to Ohio, and that if any White man carried one to that State he should give a $500 bond that the Black man should not "come upon the town" to be supported.

William Elsey Connelley, who was a strong friend of John Brown, declares in *An Appeal to the Record* that the famous "Emigrant Aid Company," which made war on Southerners in Kansas, was organized "for speculative purposes;" and Rev. Dr. Edward Everett Hale, in his *Kansas and Nebraska*, which was published in 1854, represents the movement to exclude Southerners from those territories partly, if not wholly, intended to convert them into "wealthy colonies" for the benefit of the "factories" of Massachusetts.

While Garrison's little band were sending their abolition petitions over the country and into the halls of Congress, Franklin Pierce, a Representative in Congress from New Hampshire, said in a speech delivered during the session which commenced in December, 1837: "I am unwilling that any imputation shall rest upon the North in consequence of the misguided and fanatical zeal of a few – comparatively very few – who, however honest may have been their purposes, have, I believe, done incalculable mischief and whose movements, I know, receive no more sanction at the North than they do at the South"; and as late as January, 1850, Samuel S. Phelps, a Vermont Senator, referring in a speech to what he considered unreasonable complaints on the part of Southerners, said: "As to what has been offensively said at the North, this is a land of free speech; and what is to be done with people who believe themselves charged with a mission, not only to amend the Constitution framed by the wisdom of our fathers, but also to assist the Almighty in the correction of sundry mistakes which they have discovered in His works?"

In the inaugural address of Robert J. Walker, a Pennsylvanian and an emancipationist, who had been appointed by President Buchanan Governor of Kansas, he exposed the hypocrisy of the "free-soilers" by declaring that "in their so-called Constitution, formed at Topeka, they deemed, that entire race [Negroes] so inferior and degraded as to exclude them all forever from Kansas, whether they be bond or free" – the provision having been adopted by more than four-fifths of the votes.

In the constitution of Indiana, which was adopted in 1851, after the provision that "no Negro or Mulatto shall have the right of suffrage," it is declared that "no Negro or Mulatto shall come into or settle in the State." And Indiana, be it remembered, was settled mainly by New Englanders.

Up to the time of the adoption of the 14th amendment no Colored person could vote in any Northern State east of the Hudson River, nor in Connecticut; and in the few other States where he was not absolutely disfranchised, the right to vote was practically nullified by the requirement of qualifications possessed by few Colored persons. In Massachusetts, for example, the voter had to be able to read, write, and had to own a free-hold estate "of the annual income of three pounds."

In Volume VII, for example, of John Clark Ridpath's pretentious *History of the World*, referring to this "moral awakening," he says: "The conscience of the nation" – the North being the "nation" – "was roused, and the belief began to prevail that slavery was wrong per se and ought to be destroyed," the presumption being that some competent power had authorized the "nation" to destroy it. But the books which Mr. Ridpath had studied were not written for the purpose of dealing fairly with the South, as the reader will perceive if he will examine the pages of Belford's *History of the United States*, Benton's *Thirty Years' View* and Lippincott's *Gazetteer* (1857). In these he will discover that, in a few years after the admission of Missouri, attacks on abolitionists in the North commenced, which may be summed up briefly as follows:

In 1834 an angry mob broke up the school of Prudence Crandall, in Canterbury, Connecticut, because she admitted Negro children as pupils, and destroyed valuable property. She was imprisoned in the town jail.

Just thousands of these inconsistencies can be shown, but it is needless.

CHAPTER FIVE

☆　　☆　　☆　　☆

How the North Respects Compacts

In the Convention of 1787, there was a great difference of opinion as to the powers of the Republic to be formed. The Government was to be formed of the thirteen States, then all separate distinct governments. These distinct organizations, when arising from their colonial state, had been the powers behind the Declaration of Independence which declared them to be free and independent States, each with power to do all acts and whatever else was necessary that independent and free States should do. Each had been authorized to ratify the Declaration of Independence, all acting separately.

After the war between Great Britain and the colonies, the treaty of peace with Great Britain in 1782 recognized the separate independence and sovereignty of these colonies as States. As had been done in treaties previously made with France, the Netherlands and Sweden, the States assembled through their deputies in Philadelphia to form a compact or a union more perfect and stronger than the Articles of Confederation already agreed upon. But soon the delegates found themselves contending for policies so far divergent that it looked for a time there would be no union of States. But the patriotism of the men sent by the different States to the convention prevailed, which resulted in the Constitution which was adopted by the deputies from each State. Yet each State voted as a unit. A conflict of political ideas has existed since the foundation of this nation, difference of interpretation of the Constitution has and will always exist. Parties soon sprang into existence, in creed and form. Adams and Hamilton headed one party and Thomas Jefferson the other, and these parties continued in their antagonism of views until 1861, neither party attempting to hide or disguise its construction of the Constitution. Slavery existed in all the colonies at the writing and promulgating of the Declaration of Independence, and for economic and other reasons, the North got rid of slavery, not by emancipation but by selling their slaves to the South, and the people of the North did not conclude that slavery was immoral and wrong until the industrial independence of the South threatened the political situation of the North. Then the people or leaders in the North determined to destroy the system of slavery, and no moral reason incited them to this action; it was purely political and commercial.

Now begun attacks in the pulpits of the North, in the press of the North, in Congress by Northern members, on the South, and not one word was uttered against the morality of the North selling her slave property to the South. In the most offensive language the Northern members of Congress would hold up the South and her institutions to the world, urging at all times against the South the most drastic legislation, to empower the central Government to interfere with the domestic laws of the Southern States, until the election of 1860 brought matters to a crisis. And with these brief facts let us look at some of the incidents that brought on the war of 1861-'65.

On April 1, 1783, while the Congress of the Confederation was planning at the urgent request of Northerners, to have the Articles of Confederation amended so as to substitute population for land as a basis of taxation in each State, and Southerners were objecting to New England's demand that all slaves should be included in a State's "Federal population," Mr. Gorham, of Massachusetts, gave as "a cogent reason for hastening that business, that the Eastern States, at the invitation of Massachusetts, were, with New York, about to form a Convention for regulating matters of common concern" – to violate the second clause of the 6th of the Articles of Confederation.

This threat induced the Southerners, who were anxious to perpetuate the Union, to consent to include three-fifths of the slaves in the Federal population. But when the Convention of 1787 was endeavoring to agree upon a just basis on which "representatives and direct taxes" should be apportioned among the States, New England strongly insisted that no slaves be included in the Federal population. That is to say: It was just to apportion the burdens of the members of the Confederation according to their wealth-producing power, but it was unjust to permit the Southern States to be represented in the law-making body of the Union in proportion to their wealth-producing power. And this old spirit of sectional injustice appears among the demands of the Hartford Convention.

In 1787 the famous Ordinance for the government of the Northwest Territory was adopted by eight States, and the 5,000,000 acres of land in Ohio were sold by the same States, although the pledge to the States in 1780 declared that the lands should be granted or settled "under such regulations as shall hereafter be agreed on by the United States in Congress assembled, or nine or more of them."

When Georgia and North Carolina ceded the lands which became Tennessee, Alabama and Mississippi, it was expressly agreed between them and "the United States," that "no regulations made or to be made shall tend to emancipate slaves" in the ceded territory.

When Virginia, North Carolina and Georgia made cessions of their "waste lands" one of the conditions agreed to by all parties was that these lands should be "considered as a common fund for the use and benefit" of all the States, "according to their usual respective proportions in the general charge and expenditure and shall be faithfully and bona fide disposed of for that purpose, and for no other use or purpose whatsoever." But the reports of the General Land Office show that this condition has been shamefully disregarded.

When the lands west of the Mississippi were purchased, and the taxing system of the Federal Government compelled the Southern people to contribute most of the purchase money, it cannot be claimed that it was intended or that it would be just to deny that these lands should be "considered as a common fund for the use and benefit" of all the States. But, as Senator Plumb, of Kansas, said in the United States Senate on September 25, 1888, these lands have been so disposed of as to "multiply, develop and strengthen the North."

The Constitution declares that "if a person charged in any State with treason, felony or other crime" flees to another State, the latter shall, on demand of the Governor of the injured State, surrender him; but when two of the criminals who served under John Brown when he invaded Virginia, fled, one to Ohio and the other to Iowa, the Governors of those States refused to comply with the demand of the Governor of Virginia for their surrender.

More Examples of Northern Treachery

When the "more perfect Union" was formed, each State retained what Mr. Jefferson called "interior government," and it is beyond question that the new Constitution would have been unanimously rejected it if had been expected that the Federal Government would ever assume to interfere in matters purely local, but "the North" forced the 14th amendment into the Constitution by destroying some of the States and erecting in them governments which did not represent the hereditary citizens; and this amendment subjects the States to the offensive supervision of judges who have for forty years been chosen by "the North."

The Constitution declares that "no new State shall be formed or erected within the jurisdiction of any other State;" but in 1863 thirty-nine of Virginia's counties were cut off by "the North" and erected into West Virginia.

When Thaddeus Stevens, of Pennsylvania; Zachariah Chandler, of Michigan; Benjamin F. Wade, of Ohio, and other leaders of the Republican party were balked in their scheme to degrade and insult the Southern people by inserting into the Constitution their 14th amendment, because no Southern State would consent to its own degradation, and only twenty-one of the other States were willing to assist in the disgraceful movement, these statesmen passed their "reconstruction measures," destroyed the Southern States, and erected in the borders of each what was known as a "carpet-bag government," in violation of the fundamental principles for which our forefathers contended in the Revolutionary War, in violation of well-known provisions of the Compact of Union between the States and in violation of their official oaths. Thousands of hereditary voters were disfranchised, the "carpet-bagger" who was not a citizen was given supervision of the election for members of a so-called Constitutional Convention in each province, and a ballot was placed in the hand of every Colored man (although no such persons could vote in Pennsylvania, Ohio or Michigan). Of the character of these "carpet-bag" governments the reader may get a glimpse in the following statement made by Charles Nordhoff (a Prussian) who in those days was a trusted correspondent of the *New York Herald*:

> On the other hand, the negroes and those who control their vote form a close corporation, bitterly jealous of opposition, transacting all political business by the tyrannical rule of the caucus, and ready to persecute any Republican who dares to be independent. At the first symptom of opposition to the decisions of the caucus the opposer's name is taken down; it is sent around in his county or district as that of a "bolter" and every colored voter is solemnly warned to beware of him, as though he were a rattlesnake. Men are as gravely "read out" of the Republican party in Mississippi as though it were a church; and the act of excommunication fixes, with the ignorant blacks, a stigma upon him as though he were a traitor or a murderer; and white Republican demagogues encourage this spirit of intolerance. * * * *
> As for the colored voters themselves, the testimony is universal that they are incapable of independent political action. They must have white leaders and organizers; and, under the circumstan-

ces, it is inevitable that they should fall a prey to the lowest and least scrupulous political vagabonds and demagogues. These, teach them to take up the trade of politics for a living, and tell them that, as they cast the most votes, so they are entitled to the most offices. Some of these men have not even a residence in the State. O. C. French, for instance, was at one time chairman of the Republican State Executive Committee, was appointed by Governor Ames commissioner to the Centennial Exhibition, was a representative in the Legislature from Natchez; and yet, when search was made for him the other day by a Federal law officer to enforce the penalty of a bond, he had not, so far as could be discovered, a residence in the State; and it is said and believed that he lives in Ohio.

One of the contributors to Rice's *Reminiscences*, &c., was George W. Julian, the "Free Soil" candidate for vice-president in 1852, an Indiana congressman from 1860 to 1870, and an advocate of confiscating all the property of "rebels." Discussing the issuance of Lincoln's "emancipation proclamation," he says: "Few subjects have been more debated and less understood than the Proclamation of Emancipation. Mr. Lincoln was himself opposed to the measure."

The sole object of the invasion and subjugation of the Confederate States must, therefore, have been to drive them back into the Union and keep them as "wealthy colonies;" and the time may not be far off when just men will wonder what sort of a moral code it was which held that all generations of

Southerners were bound to labor for the "prosperity" of the North because their Revolutionary ancestors carried their States into a partnership with the Northern States.

Northern Blindness to the Facts

On February 24, 1824, Thomas Jefferson addressed a letter to Jared Sparks, a New Englander, who then edited the *North American Review*, urging his plans for emancipating the slaves and deporting them to Sierra Leone; and on January 25, 1832, the Virginia House of Delegates passed a resolution declaring it "expedient to adopt some legislative enactment for the abolition of slavery."

During the session of Congress which began on the first Monday of December, 1829, Senator Thomas H. Benton, of Missouri, while the Foot resolution was being discussed, said:

> I can truly say that slavery, in the abstract, has but few advocates or defenders in the slaveholding States, and that slavery as it is, an hereditary institution, descended upon us from our ancestors, would have fewer advocates among us than it has, if those that have nothing to do with the subject would only let us alone. The sentiment in favor of slavery was much weaker before those intermeddlers began their operations than it is at present.

Searching among the most trustworthy records of the social and political institutions of ancient and mediæval nations for the causes which led to periods of exceptional moral degradation, I have been convinced by Gibbon, Milman, Hallam and others that every such period has followed and resulted from a repudiation of the popular divinities by the honored leaders of the people and the consequent weakening of the binding power of their hereditary moral code. This repudiation often, if not invariably, resulted from hostile conflicts between nations or tribes which had inherited different religious systems and worshipped different gods, and in many cases there resulted an infidelity in both combatants. The struggle to introduce Christianity into the Roman Empire, with its provinces and dependencies worshiping all sorts of gods, from a bull up to Jupiter, furnishes many illustrations of this truth; appalling pictures of depravity throughout the Byzantine empire, in France, in Asia Minor, and in some of the famous cities during three or four centuries following the decree adopting Christianity.

The census of 1850 shows that in Virginia, North Carolina, South Carolina, Georgia, Alabama and Mississippi there were 291,626 land-holders, of whom 91,797 owned no slaves. This census shows that, counting five White persons to a family, 50 per cent, of the families in these six Southern States owned no farms, and that the farmless families in Ohio were 63 per cent, of the total. Possibly the *Tribune* and Mr. Julian, if they had desired to know the truth, may have discovered that thousands of lawyers, doctors, teachers, merchants, preachers, railroad and steamboat employees, and persons engaged in other business occupations had no use for farms or slaves.

In the summer of 1863, President Lincoln and his followers in Congress cut off thirty-nine Virginia counties and admitted them into partnership with the other States as West Virginia. This was in violation of an expressed provision of that Constitution which all these statesmen had solemnly sworn to support; and if anything like this had been done in private life, the perpetrators would have been rewarded by a sojourn in some penitentiary.

Thus we have it acknowledged by the highest authority that the Republican party entered upon that career which seems to challenge formidable opposition in the Northern States, under the leadership of a man who rejected the only claim of our Revolutionary sires which the civilized world has admitted to have been a valid excuse for overthrowing British rule in the thirteen States and thus re-established so far as he could, the mediæval rule for the guidance of strong communities when dealing with weak ones; who repudiated the binding force of an official oath and thus destroyed the sanctity of a solemn appeal to the Almighty and the safeguards against perjury in courts of justice; and who taught his followers that in our dealings with our fellowmen we have no guide above expediency.

The Hon. Wm. H. Seward, Mr. Lincoln's Secretary of State, said, "There is a higher power than the Constitution which regulates our authority over domain. Slavery must be abolished and we must do it." Senator Charles Sumner, of Massachusetts, said, "The fugitive slave law is filled with horror. We are bound to disobey this act." William Lloyd Garrison said, "The Union is a lie, the American Union is an imposture, a covenant with death and agreement with hell. We are for its overthrow. Up with the flag of disunion that we may have a free republic of our own." Joshua R. Giddings said, "I look forward to the day when servile insurrection in the South will come, when the Black man, armed with British bayonets, led by British officers, shall assert his freedom and wage a war of extermination against his master." Horace Greeley said, "The Union is not worth preserving; it is not worth supporting in connection with the South." Anson P. Burlingame said, "The times demand and we must have an anti-slavery Constitution, an anti-slavery Bible and an anti-slavery God." And these same sentiments filled the abolitionist party platform that nominated Mr. Lincoln in 1860 for President of the United States.

CHAPTER SIX

☆　　☆　　☆　　☆

The Democratic Party Splits

At the opening of the 36th Congress, first session, the House stood upon roll call, 109 Republicans or Radicals to 101 Democrats, and this terrible state of affairs confronted those lovers of the Union who had hoped against hope to save the Union from the destruction this radical party was rushing it toward. The contest for Speaker of the House was closely drawn. John Sherman, of Ohio, drew to him all his party but three votes. After seven weeks of balloting without election, Sherman withdrew from the race and Wm. Pennington, of New Jersey, Republican, was elected by one vote. The Kansas and other questions were before Congress to keep in agitation the public mind. The most potent of all these was that question of squatter sovereignty. Mr. Davis offered a set of resolutions on Feb. 2, 1860, hoping to stay the dreadful result that must follow if the fanatics of the North persisted in carrying out their designs. The Northern Democrats arrayed themselves against the South on this great question with Stephen A. Douglas. Now came the Charleston convention. On April 23, 1860, the National Democratic Convention was called to order in the city of Charleston, S.C, to nominate a candidate for President. There was a wide difference of opinion in the convention on the subject of admitting slavery into the new territories. Mr. Douglas was the leader of the squatter sovereignty wing of the party. All the delegates from the North, West and South who opposed the extension of slavery flocked to the Douglas banner. The old organization, the strict constructionists of the Constitution, stood solidly for and demanded equal rights for the South under the Constitution. After the convention had gotten into working order the very first ballot disclosed the great sectional line drawn. The majority report on platform resolved that it was the duty of the Federal Government to protect all citizens in their rights of property and persons in the territories, and it was the duty of the Government to admit the territories when the State government should be lawfully organized, whether slavery should be permitted or abolished.

The minority report recognized the great difference of opinion between the two wings of the party, and resolved to abide by the decisions of the Supreme Court of the United States upon the questions of constitutional law. They thus ignored the decisions of the Supreme Court previously made and promulgated on this question, but promised to abide by some future decisions. Those who saw the animus of this minority report saw that it merely meant to differ with the majority report on all questions and stood ready to annul the opinions of the Court by one pretext or another.

The South demanded a distinct expression by the convention on this question of Supreme Court decisions; when the vote was taken some States voted as a unit, others voted by the preference of their individual delegates. Pennsylvania votes made of the minority a majority. The Cotton State delegates saw at once the inexpediency of voting that in future the Democrats would abide by the decisions of the Supreme Court. To do this was to acknowledge that the decisions of that Court already made were not final. The Cotton States refused to vote as did the Old Line Democrats and the resolution was lost. The vote of the convention to observe the two-thirds rule destroyed all Mr. Douglas' chance for the nomination, but his friends would have Douglas or nobody. On April 30, Louisiana, Alabama and Oregon withdrew from the convention. The chairman of the convention, Caleb Cushing, withdrew a part of the Massachusetts delegation. Then the convention passed a resolution to replace the delegates who left with new delegates. On May 1 Georgia withdrew from the convention. Right in this convention Massachusetts voted twenty-six times her forty-nine votes for Jefferson Davis as the Democratic party nominee for the presidency and Benj. F. Butler led this vote. No nomination was made at Charleston. On June 18 the convention adjourned to meet at Baltimore, Md.

At Baltimore the convention met again, Caleb Cushing still in the chair. Douglas was nominated by one wing of the party, Mr. Breckenridge by the other. The Republicans nominated Mr. Lincoln and over our divided house he was elected President by part of the people of the United States with the express understanding that he would rule in hostility to the South, while pretending to act as the guardian of the whole country.

Davis Elected President of the Confederacy

After Mr. Lincoln's inauguration the whole South was in a state of agitation; the fanatics of the North were urging on the destruction they desired of the Union and the constitutional right of slavery. South Carolina, in convention, seceded; then followed Mississippi. Mr. Davis then withdrew from the Senate of the United States, making one of the most pathetic appeals ever made before that body for the Union. He remained in Washington city ill for more than one week, hoping he would be arrested; that the test of the States' right to withdraw from the Union could be made before the courts. "I hope," he said to Col. Chestnut, "the President will act with moderation and will not listen to his bad advisers, the fanatics and abolitionists. If they will only give me time all is not lost. If these fanatics rule with violence on one side and extreme sense of wrong on our side the Union will be dissolved and woe must follow to the country." Mr. Davis sent telegrams and letters all over the South, begging and asking postponement of action, hoping in his love for the Union to save it from destruction and ruin. When all hope was gone Mr. Davis left Washington, his heart bowed in sorrow. He arrived in Mississippi, his home, and was appointed commander-in-chief of the State's forces and went about the work of getting the State into defensive attitude.

The Montgomery Convention met to organize the Confederate Government, elect provisional officers and do such other things as was necessary for the new government now that the war cloud had burst over the land. The South had withdrawn from the Union of States; a statesman was needed as well as a trained soldier. A man with a will to do, a soul to dare. In Mr. Davis we found the ideal man to guide the destinies of the infant republic, organize her civil departments and steer the ship clear of the rocks and breakers of those turbulent times. By common assent all the delegates assembled in convention at Montgomery, Ala., chose Mr. Davis as the best-fitted man as first President of the young Confederacy. In 1862 he was elected by the votes of all people of the seceding States constitutional President of the Confederate States of America.

Positively, Mr. Davis did not seek the position; the position sought him. After the State of Mississippi seceded from the Union, Mr. Davis was appointed by the Governor commander-in-chief of the State forces, and he was as much astonished as man could be when the Montgomery convention chose him President. It is absurd for the writers and historians of the North to insist, as they do, that Mr. Davis was the choice of the politicians and not of the whole people of the South. He was absolutely the people's choice. It is true the movement of the South in 1861 was sudden and it was intense, but it was not the work of politicians; it was the action of a people who had been rudely awakened from their dream of security. A great danger presented itself to the whole South. A necessity for quick action confronted the people. Their liberty and happiness were threatened by the fanatics who had gotten control of the Government power, and these people left the South but one course; that was separation from the Union of States.

When Mr. Davis received official notice of his appointment as provisional President of the Confederacy, as I said before, he was astonished, and had he followed the bent of his own inclination he would have declined the honor; but his loyalty to the South, his love of the people, his devotion to duty, made him cast aside all thoughts of self and surrender himself to the good of his people and his beloved South. And I want to impress upon the generation of today this fact: We of the past know it is true, that Jefferson Davis was the most unselfish patriot and friend that ever lived – gentle in manner, kind in disposition, with an open hand of charity for all who needed his help, with a devotion to duty, with faith in God's help, Jefferson Davis was the ideal man of his day.

The War Comes at Last

After Mr. Davis was inaugurated President of the Confederate States, so great was his love for the Union and its perpetuation and his hope that no blood would be shed, he carried out and appointed the peace commission as authorized by the Provisional Congress. This commission was composed of the South's best and patriotic citizens: A. B. Roman, Louisiana; Martin J. Crawford, Georgia; John B. Forsyth, Alabama. The political views of these gentlemen had no weight with Mr. Davis in making the appointments. Judge Roman of Louisiana, was a Whig; Mr. Crawford, Georgia, a States' rights Democrat; and Mr. Forsyth an ardent and zealous Douglas man. He gave them no instructions but left all to their patriotism and honest conviction of right, and this alone was their guide. But nothing came of this attempt on the part of the South to prevent bloodshed. This commission went to Washington city and were deceived to such an extent by the new President's advisors, the fanatical leaders of the North that had determined upon war and only war, they left in sorrow when their last hope of peace had fled. I cannot go into details of this story of deception and fraud played upon our commission by Mr. Lincoln and his Cabinet to gain time; it is obtainable by all who care to read it.

War was now upon us. Its iron hand was raised to crush the Confederacy. All promises had been broken by the Northern leaders; the tie that bound us as a union broken by the treachery of the fanatical North. Mr. Lincoln had called for troops to coerce the South back into an unbearable union. On May 6, 1861, the Army of the Confederate States was lawfully established in lieu of the provisional army, and war was on.

"No man," said an eminent writer, "unless it was Washington, was ever placed in a position so fraught with danger, so burdened with cares and responsibilities, as was Mr. Davis when he became President of the Confederacy." With this writer I most heartily concur and go further and say no man could have filled the position and performed the duties of the office better than Mr. Davis. His name will be revered by all Southern men, women and children. His place will be high upon the scroll of fame; no name will be written in truthful history above that of Mr. Davis. His grand character, genial nature, honesty of purpose, adherence to principle, made him the idol of our people. And the day will come when in the whole country Jefferson Davis will be held as the greatest American patriot that ever lived.

We can fully understand why the press, the pulpit and the historians of the North slander Mr. Davis. They are paid for it. Whatever slander is put forth by the press, pulpit or speaker of the North is taken by the Northern people as gospel truth. These people do not want the truth; they don't care for it. But I cannot understand how any man who wore the gray coat of the Confederacy and honestly believed in the principle for which he fought can ever harshly criticize Mr. Davis' work as President of the Confederate States. We grant it that Mr. Davis' public life is public property and every man has a right to his personal opinion. But whenever a Confederate soldier speaks lightly of President Davis and questions his acts as President of the Confederacy, he puts it into the power of our enemies to say we had not the faith we professed in our leader nor our cause. It is a fact that all the criticisms made of Mr. Davis and his work, as a rule, are made in total ignorance of the facts and conditions that surrounded the case upon which he acted and with which so much fault is found by his critics. We have often heard Mr. Davis blamed in the most senseless manner by people who have nothing better upon which to base their criticisms than some slanderous article they read in a newspaper, novel or magazine. These people do not inform themselves yet they loudly proclaim. "They pin their opinions to no man's coat sleeve" and yet they will base an opinion upon some very irresponsible Northern publication.

But the climax of bosh is to blame Mr. Davis for the failure of the Confederacy to establish its independence. If those people who blame him would simply read current history they would soon discover how little they knew about the real cause of the Confederacy's collapse. No man, we do not care who he might have been nor what may have been his ability, had he been in the Presidential chair of the Confederacy in 1864-'65 could have done more than Mr.

Davis did do to avert the end and change the result. No power on earth, no power but that of God's, could have stayed the collapse of the Confederacy after those twin monsters, hunger and starvation, forced our gates. These monsters hastened the end.

"The dark shadows of slander always follow the defeated and the leaders of a defeated cause are always the victims;" they must suffer. Their wisest counsel, their purest motives are distorted by slander and misrepresentation into acts of treachery to the people and the cause they love. The most self-sacrificing acts are made by slander and misrepresentation to look like the blackest villainies, and it is a well-known fact that there have been men who wore the garb of the Confederate soldier that dared to impugn and misrepresent Robert E. Lee. How then was it possible for Mr. Davis to escape the malignity of the tongues that would assail Lee, the purest character the world has ever known. Slander and hatred were not born in 1861-'65; nor was their birthplace the South. These monsters began their existence at the birth of time. The history of all nations, the history of all people who fail in the cause of right or wrong is their leaders must suffer and the South was no exception to this rule. No man has yet been able to point out one act of President Davis during his term of office that can be tortured or twisted into the cause of our failure. There was a multiplicity of causes combined that brought about the collapse of our cause, and I think it can truthfully be said that none of all the causes were so potent as those of hunger and starvation. God alone could have controlled these and averted the end.

The Cause of the South was Just

We would ask this of every man who wore the gray: Do you believe because we failed to establish our independence that our cause was unholy, unrighteous, unjust and the principles for which we fought unpatriotic? If you do believe these things take off that gray coat, the emblem of the past. It is the emblem of a principle that made you a traitor to your manhood, a traitor to your God. The principles for which we fought and defended our homes are as holy and just today as they were in 1861-'65. They can never die. The cause was truth itself. We were right in 1861, we are right now, although right is strangled by illegal amendments to the Constitution, enacted by a Congress filled with carpet-baggers, scallywags and tramps, who had not the right of citizenship in the Southern States by birth nor residence. Do not all these truths prove that when Mr. Seward spoke of the higher power that regulated the power of his party over domain was the law of might – the law which disregards the divine law and ignores justice and truth?

I want to call your attention to a misstatement of a fact continually made by the Northern people and often by our own people, i.e., that the South submitted her cause to the arbitration of the sword; she lost, and lost her right of appeal. This statement of our case is false, in fact, it is false in construction, it is false in law. We did not submit our cause to the arbitration of war. We left the Union of States, exercising the legal right given us by the Constitution, and simply asked to be let alone. When armed forces invaded our States and threatened our homes, we took up arms in defense of our loved ones and our legal rights, and exercised the divine right of self-protection and self-preservation as free American citizens. This, I say, is the correct statement of our position in 1861-'65, and this will be our true position in the truthful history of those times. We were outnumbered and overpowered and we are willing to accept the results; but we must not be asked or expected to say our cause was unholy or unpatriotic and our leaders traitors. In the light of events since the close of the Civil War, I think it is clear to all honest men that the South was right in her position of 1861-'65 and is still right.

Facts are daily coming to the surface that should prove to those who care for truth in history, that it would have been just as impossible for the Confederacy to have succeeded under any other leadership as it was under the leadership of Mr. Davis. We were shut in from all commerce with the outer world; now and then a blockade runner entered our ports and brought us word from the outer world. We had no navy. Within our gates was a relentless enemy, the Union man, who let no opportunity pass to convey to the enemy outside our position. We were surrounded by a well-armed, well-fed, well-clothed army, that outnumbered us two to one. Our army was poorly armed, illy fed and badly clothed. If we lost a man it was a gap in the ranks we could not fill. Yet we had the courage of conviction that our cause was just, but I say again of all the factors so potent in the collapse of our cause, none were so potent as the starvation of our troops and people. Human nature could not have done more than we did do to avert the end, and I honestly say if it had not been for the guiding hand of Jefferson Davis upon the helm of the ship of state and the invincible sword of Robert E. Lee at the head of our army, our Appomattox would have come long before it did.

When the end came Mr. Davis was made the victim of the slander and hatred of the Northern pulpit and press. Behind these stood the fanatical politicians, vying with each other in slandering our leader and our people. This was the part of their scheme to hide from the masses the treasure and lives it had cost the North to accomplish the robbery of the legal rights of the people of the South.

Mr. Davis was arrested, confined in a cell at Fortress Monroe, ironed like a criminal by Gen. Nelson A. Miles, unable to eat the coarse food given him, unable to sleep because of the constant tramp of the guard in his cell. What cruel, inhuman treatment, inflicted upon this broken old man, whose only crime was his love of liberty, justice, truth and patriotism; kept in this cell, denied even the necessities of life for so long a time that even his very torturers became ashamed of their cruelty and released him on a bond. They indicted him for treason and then dared not try him before their venal courts, packed as they were by men who would have willingly obeyed any inhuman order of a corrupt Government. Yea, gladly would these creatures of a fanatical power have hung Mr. Davis. Their cruel cowardly cry for his life will stand forever a stain upon that party made great by Lincoln's name.

After Mr. Davis was released from prison he lived amongst the people of his beloved South, persecuted by a vindictive Government he helped to make great. He was deprived of citizenship; robbed of all civil rights. He was a man without a country, yet he had a country. It was in the hearts of the Southern people. In that country he was the uncrowned king. If the people of the South or the Confederate soldier ever forgets the sacrifices made by Jefferson Davis for them, then, indeed, will come the second apostacy of man upon earth. Ingratitude will take the place of virtue and the story of 1861-'65 will cease to be told. It will be blotted from the record forever. But this will never be. When the bar of truthful history shall judge Mr. Davis and his work, the verdict will be written – Jefferson Davis, the American patriot, whose adherence to principle, fortitude under trial, fidelity to duty, rectitude of private and public life, the martyr to the cause of justice and truth. In life slander did not smirch him; it cannot reach him now.

It is the duty of every man who loves the South and her treasured memories of the past to teach the generation of today the truthful side of our cause and our part in the great struggle of right against might. Teach the young generation of today the causes that led up to the war. This is far more important than the history of our battles that every schoolboy is familiar with. Let the truth be told that our boys and girls may fully understand our side of the great question and be able to intelligently defend our names when we have passed over into the camp grounds of eternity. There should be no untruthful history taught in our schools. All histories that are not truthful and fair should be banished. Every home, every library, every school in the South should have a copy of Mr. Davis' work, *The Rise and Fall of the Confederate Government*. This should be the text-book of our public schools and not the unfair, untruthful histories that are used to-day. We should put into the hands of our young people Mr. Davis' work as we put into their hands the Bible. It is a book that all Southern men and women can feel proud of. It is a book of which no honest American citizen should feel ashamed. It is a work stamped with true statesmanship, filled with patriotism. It is a clear, concise, truthful statement of the whole question and all facts as they existed before and during the war of 1861-'65.

I do not claim for Mr. Davis infallibility nor impeccability. He was human like you and I. He made some mistakes and committed some errors that may look very gigantic to us without the facts of the case before us; when, in truth, if we had all the facts, we would more than likely praise as wisdom that which we now condemn as folly. Human nature cannot be perfect nor can all men agree upon questions of public and private character, and yet men can be honest in their views and convictions: but I am forced to say, after a careful study of all the questions bearing on the great conflict, that I cannot concede to the leaders of the fanatical parties of the North of 1861-'65 one particle of honesty in their attitude toward the South. Commercialism, greed and envy has much to do with their opinions. Their love of humanity and the Negro was simply cant and hypocrisy of the most flimsy character. What they deny the Negro in Massachusetts they insist he shall have in the South. We had the Negro laborer; the North would have him free; not to help the Negro, but to cripple the industries of the South and to keep, if possible, the Radical Party in power by the Negro vote. Thank God, we had a people war could not destroy; cruelty nor persecution could not make them forget their past and its glories; can we ever forget the list of crimes committed against our liberty, that forced upon us the calamity of war and the days of reconstruction?

I repeat that the Negro was but one factor in the war. Beyond him was the great principle of States' rights, of which Mr. Davis was always the South's champion and which Blaine and Sherman claimed for their States, and California and Nevada claims today. When we formed the Confederacy we placed upon Mr. Davis' shoulders the toga of the Presidency as the best fitted man to guide our ship of state through the turbulent sea of political turmoil and war. He did not seek the office. The office was forced upon him; honestly, faithfully, ably and patriotically he performed the duties imposed upon him by the people and for their best interests. Cruelty and persecution could not weaken his great love for humanity nor swerve him from liberty's cause. His greatness of soul was beyond the small things of life. The great men of the times, said an eminent English prelate, are always a helpless mark for the coarse lies and vulgarity of a peering malice; the sad, weak breath of envy always wounds those that attain distinction. Fame cannot escape slander. Greatness of soul cannot escape envy, and Jefferson Davis was not an exception to this rule.

But I would say this to all men who wore the gray, do not be led away to harshly criticise Mr. Davis. It is your bounded duty to hold up to the youth of today the character of Jefferson Davis as a model for them. And I say without fear of contradiction if they will investigate for themselves his private and public life they will find a gentle, pure heart, a great soul, that was filled with love for God and his country.

Let no man who wore the gray forget himself ever to descend into the mire of slander and hate with the enemies of our beloved leader. All that has been uttered by the pulpit, press and people of the North against Mr. Davis is but assertion. This is not proof; abuse is not demonstration. That which we have claimed for him stands boldly out before the world, sustained by justice and supported by the staff of truth. It stands unbent beneath the mountain of errors and misrepresentation hurled against him by malice and hate. His was the soul that never forgot its greatness. His was the manhood that never forgot its duty to God nor man. His was the heart filled with Christian charity as the Master taught, and I do believe as implicitly as I believe in a future that Jefferson Davis surrendered back to his Creator an unspotted soul, unsmirched by treachery or deceit. The bright dawn of the day that is to proclaim Jefferson Davis the greatest of American patriots is almost here; the points of the bright sun are coming up out of the night of malice and slander; it will burst over the world to set no more. All the world will love Jefferson Davis' name as we of the South always have and will.

These facts presented to our children and the world are not exaggerated nor distorted to meet our case. They are the historical facts that cannot be blotted out nor erased from American history.

PART II
The Confederate Soldier

Robert E. Lee

CHAPTER SEVEN

☆　　☆　　☆　　☆

The Ideal Soldier of the World

The history of every nation is written upon its battlefields. The history of the Confederate States was written in 1861-'65, upon the battle plains of the South. Fame then wrote upon her scroll in the indelible ink of glory the name and valor of every Confederate soldier who wore the gray and did his duty to his State in obedience to her laws.

When the American colonies began their struggle to take from the King of England the power of government and transfer it to the people of the colonies, there was gathered and mustered an invincible army of patriots. They were banded together in Liberty's holy name. No such army was needed again, no such army was gathered again, until 1861, when the Southern States were compelled to protect themselves against the flagrant usurpation of power and the open violation of their constitutional rights by the fanatical party that had become possessed of the government reins. It became necessary for the

South and her people to gather and organize an army to protect our homes and our legal rights. The necessity was urgent, and from this urgent necessity was born the Confederate Army.

This army of Confederate Patriots was just as invincible on the field of battle as was the Colonial Army of 1776. And I here make this claim – that the army of 1861-'65 was not conquered by the army of coercion sent by the fanatics of the North against us. We were defeated by that monster – starvation – the foe whose strength conquers the bravest.

The Confederate Army was a gathering of ideal soldiers. No such army will ever again be gathered, unless collected from the sons of the men in gray of 1861-'65. It was composed of the intelligence and valor of the South, and I do not believe there ever was collected upon the face of the earth men that possessed to a greater degree the essentials to the making of good soldiers as did the Confederate recruits of 1861.

The essentials necessary to the making of good soldiers are intelligence, obedience and courage. Courage without the force of intelligence to direct it counts for very little in battles. An army may be ever so brave, but, if it lacks intelligence, it cannot win victories from its more intelligent foes.

It is conceded by all military students that the raw Confederate recruit of 1861 developed into an efficient soldier more rapidly than any other man known to military history; and this same authority agrees that the Confederate Army's intelligence, obedience and courage was of the highest order. This was the power that made the Confederate soldier so effective and so destructive of his opponents upon the battlefield. I shall make this claim, that the Confederate Army of 1861-'65 was the grandest army ever organized, and the Confederate soldier the ideal soldier of the world; the most intelligent, obedient and courageous the world has ever known. He was also the most destructive. His intelligence to understand all orders given him by his commander, his obedience and courage to execute the order made the man in gray the effective fighter he was. And this combination of the essentials made the old "Reb" of 1861-'65 invincible whenever and wherever he was not outnumbered upon the field of battle.

There was another essential we had beyond the three named. We had the absolute conviction that, in the sight of God and man, our cause was just, legal and holy. Guided by such conviction, backed by manhood, honor and right, could the Confederate soldier have been other than he was – the ideal soldier of the world. He loved his home, the land of his birth; he obeyed the laws, and was ever ready to defend them. He did not fight for gold. He fought in defence of his home. He fought for a principle which was honor, justice and truth combined. These are the principles that make heroes of nations. These principles made heroes of the men in gray who from 1861-'65 were down in the mud and toted the gun.

I do not intend, in this paper, to refer in an extended way to our grand commanders who led us through the struggle. They have had their full share of praise and glory. Their names and their deeds will live forever. They deserve all the glory that has been showered upon them by the world. It is theirs by right; no power on earth can tear one leaf from their laurel-crowned brows.

I want to talk tonight of the man who was down in the mud, the man in the ranks, the man who tramped under the burning sun, the man who faced the cold of winter, barefooted and almost naked, and carried the gun; the man whose intelligence, obedience and courage during the four long years of bloody war made it possible for Robert E. Lee and the immortal "Stonewall" Jackson to plan the battles and win victories from armies double their numbers. To the man who marched down in the mud, badly armed, poorly clad, oftimes hungry, certainly belongs part of the glory of the past. He won it; he deserves it. Grand old hero in gray! Your intelligence, obedience and courage made you the wonder of the world. You never were driven from the battlefield in panic and rout. If you were it was caused by the blundering of your officers and was not your fault. A grand army was the Confederate army; a wonderful soldier was the man in gray. Guided by the wisdom of Lee, led by the genius of Jackson, aided by the dash of Stuart, Ashby and the noble others who wore the gray, you often grasped victory from the enemy when defeat seemed inevitable.

The record shows that you never fought one battle during the whole war that your opponents did not outnumber you, two to one, often five to one. The Union Army was always better armed than we were. They were better clothed, always well fed, and never failed to have an abundance of the best ammunition. In fact, they had nothing that was necessary to make an army effective that money could purchase, and yet with all this advantage in equipment and numbers, you, with your old flintlock gun, often drove them from the field of battle in panic and rout.

We did not have the improved guns of that day, nor the good rations, clothing and ammunition. But we had something better than all these. We had the absolute conviction that our cause was just and holy, and this gave the Confederate soldier the moral and physical courage, the strength that $13 per month and the best of rations cannot give.

We often hear the question asked, but never by a Confederate soldier, why it was that "Stonewall" Jackson so often disregarded all rules of military science as taught in the books, flinging them aside and fighting battles under conditions from which most military leaders would retreat! This question can be readily answered by any man who followed old "Stonewall" up and down the Valley. And the answer is this: "Stonewall" Jackson had implicit faith in his men in the ranks and these men had blind confidence in him; they implicitly trusted him and he knew he was backed in any move he might make by the man who carried the gun, who would fully understand all orders given him. And "Stonewall" Jackson also knew that his men in the ranks had the obedience and courage to execute all orders given them, hence Jackson could fling aside the laws of the books, for he felt perfectly safe in facing double his numbers and defeating armies, which he repeatedly did, five times his number. It is now admitted that "Stonewall" Jackson and his men never fought one battle in the Valley that he was not compelled to fight double his numbers. And with Jackson, the rule was to make the enemy fight or retreat wherever he met them, no matter how superior might be their numbers to his own.

Facts Drawn From the Official Record

I am going to prove my claim for the man in gray, who was down in the mud, by the reports of the Adjutant-General, U.S.A., 1861-'65. A study of these reports will interest those who care to read them. It will convince those who choose to investigate, that, in every battle fought between the Confederate Army and the Union Army, 1861-'65, the Union Army always outnumbered the Confederate forces two to one, often five to one; and, notwithstanding the "Yanks" had more men, better guns, surer and better ammunition, they never drove us from the field in panic and rout as we often drove them. I do not deny the fact that we were sometimes compelled to fall back, and, in doing so, we lost guns and men. But I do say we never ran in panic and rout; never lost our organization as an army to such an extent that the enemy felt safe in following us in our retreats. But this you will bear me out in saying, that the Federal Army did more than once repeat its rout and panic of 1861 of Manassas field.

And this is one of the confirmations of my claim for the Confederate soldier that he was the ideal soldier of the world; the fighting soldier without an equal. He was cool in action, steady under fire, never losing his head. He understood his duty, he knew what was expected of him, and he never disappointed his officers. His old gray jacket was the emblem of his cause; it was his badge of nobility; his pride, his honor was concentrated in his love for the cause; death could not make him sacrifice it.

And let me say right here, whenever you come in contact with a man, even at this day, who is not proud of the fact that he honorably wore that old gray jacket, mud-bespattered as it was, you can put it down as a certainty he was not much in love with the cause in those days of blood. There are but few men, thank God, who wore the gray that are ashamed to proclaim it today. I say we were right in 1861-'65; we are right today. I sometimes hear men say, "We thought we were right." That is not the proper way to put it.

I say, before God and man, I absolutely know the principle for which we fought was holy, just and legal, and we must always say so. If there is a Confederate veteran living today who cannot look the world in the face and say from the depths of his heart that he was right, his cause patriotic and just, he should take off his coat of gray, bury it beneath the sod, and over its grave write, "Here lies buried the emblem of the principle that led me astray, made me untrue to my God and myself, made me a traitor to my country, made me battle for a principle I did not believe." Can you, comrades, say this? I know you cannot and I know you will not.

Now, the record – I wish to call your especial attention to figures to sustain my claim for the men in gray. These figures are taken from the official Army Reports of the United States and Confederate States, which are in the possession of the War Department at Washington. Remember these figures, tell them to your children's children, teach them to the generation of today, that they may not be forgotten when you and I have passed away. These facts, these figures will enable our children to tell our story with pride and without shame. They can say, "My father followed Lee and Jackson and the flag of the Confederate States, whither it led, unto the end. Their cause was the cause of liberty, as holy and just as men ever battled for in Liberty's sacred name.

The historians of the North have not been idle since the close of the great struggle in writing what they claim is fair and impartial history of 1861-'65, and I, regret to say, some of these perverted and false histories have found place in our public and private schools of the South. The most of these histories, if not all, say the South and her soldiers fought solely for the enslavement of the Negro, and that no other principle was involved. I will show you how the facts and figures completely refute this slander, and I believe the date I give you is near absolutely correct.

For every one hundred White citizens in the South in 1861, there were but four that owned slave property. There were enlisted into the Confederate Army, during the four years of war, 639,000 men, all told. Of this number, you will see, there were but 200,000 who owned slave property. If this be true (and it *is* true) I would ask these historical slanderers of the South this question: If there were but 200,000 slave-owners in the Confederate Army, in the name of common sense, what were the other 400,000 fighting for? Surely not for fun. War is not fun. There is no fun in killing, and war means killing. It means death in all its horrible forms. It means suffering, pain and want. It means all the ills that can be inflicted upon humanity, and surely there is no pleasure in the inhumanity that follows in the wake of war; I care not how humanely it may be conducted.

There was a principle involved in that great struggle of '61-'65; a principle these slanderers do not want the world to see. It was a principle beyond that of Negro slavery. We fought for the preservation of the Constitution and the guaranteed rights of all citizens. This was the paramount issue of the war and these slanderers of the South and her people know it. And when they admit this truth their cause is lost and the South is vindicated before the world; and this these perverters of truth do not intend to happen if they can prevent it. We stood in 1861-'65 for this great principle; we were the true defenders of the Constitution then; we are its defenders now, and the world today concedes that the Confederate soldier was the true, honest patriot, the real defender of the Constitution and Republican form of government intended by the builders of this great Nation.

Now let me get back to the figures and the man in gray. During the four years of war ('61-'65) the Confederate Army fought 2,261 battles. This does not include skirmishes and minor engagements; 521, or 25 per cent, of these battles were fought on Virginia soil. In 1861, the Confederate armies fought 150 battles; in 1862, 564; in 1863, 627; in 1864, 779; in 1865, 135.

The Census of 1860 shows a population in the Northern States, subject to military duty, of 4,500,000. In the South, or properly the Thirteen Original Seceding States, a population of 1,046,000. The Adjutant-General's Report (United States Army, 1861-'65) says there were recruited into the United States Army, during the four years of war, 2,553,062 men of all arms. A corrected report and later figures say there were 2,800,000 and this figure, I think, is correct. Here, by their own report, taking their own figures, they began the war and they led at all times, four men to our one. The very highest estimate ever put upon the Confederate Army in four years, all told, has been 639,000 men of all arms. We had in the field all our available men; we could get no more; while the Union Army could and *did* recruit from all parts of the globe. From Germany, if we can take the troops they had in this Valley as a guide, they obtained most of their recruits. I have seen men in this Valley in blue uniforms who could not tell their names and regiments in English to save their lives. Every man who followed "Stonewall" Jackson knows this is true. These foreigners wore the blue and were counted Yankee soldiers.

It was not only from the European countries that the Federal armies were recruited, but they enlisted men from the Border and from the Seceding States. The Adjutant-General's Report (United States Army) shows Maryland furnished 53,316 White troops; 32,068 came from what is now West Virginia; from Kentucky, 79,025; Missouri, 169,111; South Carolina, 15,000: while North Carolina, Mississippi, Tennessee, Florida, and Louisiana all furnished White troops to the Yankee Army. This report of the Adjutant-General shows this fact – that the Union Army recruited from the Thirteen Original Seceding States 300,000 White troops, just half as many men as we had in our army at any time.

In plainer terms, the Confederate Army recruited 639,000 men; the Union Army 300,000 traitors. When we stop to consider this traitor force within our gates, combined with that monster – starvation – is it not wonderful that we held out as long as we did? These figures, I think, go far to support my claim for the Confederate men in the ranks who were down in the mud. He was the grandest soldier the world ever knew. The man that toted the gun was the ideal soldier with which no other nation's soldiers can compare.

Here is an extract from what C.B. Anderson

says in his book, *Fighting By Southern Federals*, and I use it for what it is worth. If it is true, and he claims to have data to prove it, then it is strange we lasted as long as we did:

> Who would suppose that Louisiana furnished more soldiers to the Union armies in the war between the States than did Rhode Island; that Virginia furnished 37,791 Federal soldiers, while Minnesota furnished 24,020; that Tennessee furnished 51,225 and New Hampshire only 33,937; that Kentucky furnished more than Maine and Missouri more than Wisconsin?

The evidence Mr. Anderson provides appears to justify the claim. He says there were 634,255 Southern-born men who fought against the South and for the preservation of the Union, divided as follows: Two hundred and ninety-six thousand, five hundred and seventy-eight White men from Southern States, 137,676 Colored men living in the South and approximately 200,000 men living in the North who were born in the South. He says many officers who rendered distinguished service in the Federal Army were natives of the South. He gives their names and the positions they held. Among them were 160 brigadier-generals. There were 4,000 commissioned officers from Kentucky in the Federal Army. Is it any wonder the South lost the war?

The author has brought out many interesting facts concerning the war never before published. He has reviewed the entire war period, mentioning important events as they occurred day by day and vividly describing the famous engagements. The volume fills an important place in Civil War history.

A word or two on pensions to corroborate further my claim for the Confederate soldier, for all I shall say goes in as proof positive of the claim. The Commissioner of Pensions in his last Report says that since the close of the war (1861-'65) the United States Government has paid to the United States soldiers of 1861-'65, their widows and dependents, $4,073,816,352.89, total 1909 to July, 1910. This does not include salaries nor expenses in keeping and maintaining Soldiers' Homes. The number of cases, says the same Report, now pending and awaiting settlement under the General Pension Laws, is 137,201, and those pensions that come under the act of June 27, 1890, number 142,679. The average value of each pension is $132. This pension list forms the great bulk of our public debt, and of this vast sum – $4,073,816,352.89 – the South has paid and is still paying in taxes one-third of the amount from which we derive no benefit.

The Confederate soldier's family was robbed by the soldiers of the Union Army during the war; they were plundered by the carpet-baggers during the days of reconstruction, and we are bowed down now paying taxes to pension a lot of camp-followers and villains who never fired a gun nor stood in the line of battle. Notwithstanding the fact that this gigantic pension list shows the fighting ability of the Confederate soldier, we find it questioned by men in the North who persist in the slander that the old

"Reb" of 1861-'65 would not and did not fight.

The Payment of Pensions

Here is a very interesting statement made by the *Baltimore Sun*, July 10th, on pensions. Washington, D.C, July 10:

The cost of the nation's wars in pensions alone has been more than $4,000,000,000. With the close of the fiscal year 1910, on June 30, figures were available showing that the four-billion-dollar mark has been passed during the past twelve months.

The total disbursements for pensions from the beginning of the Government to June 30, 1909, is given by the Pension Office as $3,913,082,-513.73. The statement of the United States Treasury issued on July 1, shows that the total disbursements for pensions during the fiscal year ended last Thursday was $160,733,839.16. These latter figures are unrevised, but when finally made up will run a fraction larger than the sum given. The amount carried in the Pension Appropriation bill for the fiscal year 1910 was $160,908,000, so that the amount actually disbursed runs very close to the appropriations made. This gives a grand total of $4,073,816,352.89 spent on pensions to soldiers, sailors and marines, their widows, minor children and dependent relatives.

Cost Millions to Pay Them.

This does not include the cost of maintenance and expenses connected with the payment of pensions. Between 1866 and June 30, 1909, the amount spent for maintenance of the system – wholly aside from the payment of pensions – was $115,705,060.82, which, added to the aggregate paid for pensions, brings the grand total cost of the pension system up to $4,189,521,413.71 to June 30, 1910.

The amount disbursed from pensions from the Revolution to June 30, 1865, was $96,445,-444.23. The amount disbursed for pensions since the Civil War, exclusive of cost of administration, has been $3,977,370,908.66, and including the cost of administration $4,093,075,969.48 – 40 times as great during the past 45 years as during the previous 75 years.

What Wars Have Cost.

The amounts paid for pensions to soldiers, sailors and their dependents from the foundation of the Government to date may be shown as follows:

War of the Revolution	$70,000,000.00
War of 1812	45,757,396.84
Indian wars	9,995,609.47
War with Mexico	42,492,784.07
Civil War	3,686,461,840.35
War with Spain and Philippine Insurrection	26,383,805.21
Regular establishment	15,507,028.02
Unclassified	16,484,049.77

Total to June 30, 1909	$3,913,082,513.73
Total 1909 to July 1, 1910	160,733,839.16

Total for pensions to date . . . $4,073,816,352.89
Administrative cost 1865-1909 .115,705,060.82

Grand total to date $4,189,521,413.17

Started at $15,000,000 a Year.

The total amount spent on the pension system during the first year after the Civil War was $15,857,714.88, and the cost of administration during the fiscal year 1866 was only $417,165. There were then only 126,722 pensioners on the rolls. Since that time the number of pensioners has rapidly increased, until it now hovers around the million mark, the number on the rolls on June 30, 1909, having been 946,194, of which pensions are paid to 632,557 persons on account of the Civil War. The distribution of these pensioners according to the wars, as given by the latest available table is as follows:

Revolutionary War 1
War of 1812 395
Indian wars 4,625
Mexican War 9,092
Civil War 888,690
Spanish War 7,095
Regulars 16,296

946,194

The distribution of the pensioners as to survivors, widows, etc., according to the latest available figures, is as follows:

Invalid and aged survivors 632,557
Widows 298,853
Children 4,971
Mothers 7,016
Fathers 1,176
Brothers, sisters, etc. 295
Helpless children 848
                                    ———————
                                      946,194

Only 593,961 of Them Veterans.

These tables show that while there are 888,690 persons being pensioned on account of the Civil War, that the actual number of survivors of the war on the pension list was 593,961, the rest of the Civil War pensioners being distributed among the classes of army and navy widows, children and other dependents. For the Civil War this distribution was as follows:

Survivors 593,961
Widows 285,137
Minor children 4,508
Mothers 2,996
Fathers 493
Brothers, etc. 280
Helpless children 837
Army nurses 478
                                    ———————
                                      888,690

The total amount paid during the fiscal year 1909 to these 888,690 Civil War pensioners was $152,868,814.40, leaving $9,104,889.37 distributed on account of other wars. The total paid to the regular establishment was $2,879,080.14, to pensioners of the Spanish-American War, $3,820,-169.80; to pensioners of the Mexican War, $1,678,-636.57 and to Indian war pensioners, $639,898.44.

Laws by Which They are Paid.

Under the Age Pension law of 1907, $58,-383,177.88 was paid during the fiscal year 1909 to survivors of the war over 62 years of age, while $34,637,978.20 was paid to Civil War survivors under the general disability laws, and $16,276,-650.34 was paid to Civil War survivors under the act of 1890. More than $42,000,000 was paid during that year to widows of soldiers and sailors of the Civil War. Under the general law $12,270,711 was paid to Civil War widows, children and dependents, while the act of 1908, which increased the pensions to army and navy pensioners, resulted in an additional expenditure of $30,-278,825.35 for widows.

From 1900 to 1904, inclusive, the number of certificates of pension issued was 621,842. From 1905 to 1909, inclusive, the number issued, not including 202,577 increases under the act of 1908 made by direction of former Commissioner of Pensions Warner to pension agents on the original certificates of the pensioners in order to save the pensioners the trouble and expense of filing applications therefor, was 1,011,082. This was an increase of 389,240 as compared with the previous five years.

From 1900 to 1904, inclusive, pensions

amounting to $693,351,107.68 were paid. From 1905 to 1909, inclusive, there was paid as pensions $733,365,352.08 so that the latter five-year period represents an increase of $40,014,244.40 in pension expenditures as compared with the five years of the decade. The year 1910 starts over another five-year period with an expenditure of $160,-733,839. The amount appropriated by the last Congress in the Pension bill for the fiscal year 1911 just begun is $155,758,000, to which must be added an increase of approximately $2,000,000 authorized by some 6,100 special private pension acts.

Takes Half Tariff to Pay It.

Indications are that during the five-year period from 1910 to 1914, inclusive, the expenditure for pensions will be around $750,000,000 if not more, or nearly enough to build the Panama Canal twice, according to the original estimates of the engineers. The total amount spent on the construction of the canal to June 30, 1910, was $204,096,-342.07. The amount paid for pensions during the year just closed and to be spent during the fiscal year 1911, just begun, will aggregate more than $300,000,000.

This amount represents almost the entire customs revenue of the country in a single year. During the fiscal year which ended June 30, 1910, the aggregate amount collected from customs, the country's greatest single source of revenue, was $332,785,323.27. During the fiscal year 1909 the country's revenue from customs, under the Dingley law, was $300,711,933.95.

The Death Rates Compared

Let us now look into another proof of the Confederate soldier's claim to first rank. If the death-rate of army is to be taken as our guide and proof of the fighting ability of an army, the Confederate Army takes first rank, for it is a fact, conceded and proven by the Record that the Confederate armies often, in battle, destroyed more than one-fourth of the enemy engaged. History furnishes no record of soldiers that will compare with the man in gray, who went into the fight with a flintlock gun and armed himself with the gun of his opponent.

Now, we look into the regimental losses and see what they show. All these figures are official, taken from the reports. In the battle of Gettysburg, the 26th North Carolina Infantry lost 90 per cent. of its number engaged. This regiment went into the fight with 800 muskets strong and lost 558 men, killed and wounded. The survivors joined the Pickett charge and lost in killed and wounded all but 80 men. Such regimental loss as this was never known before nor since Gettysburg. The 1st Maryland Confederate Regiment, and there was none better in the army, lost of its numbers engaged 82 per cent.; the 21st Georgia lost 76 per cent.; the 6th Mississippi, 71 per cent.; the 5th Texas, 82 per cent. These losses show, at least, if nothing else, stubborn fighting qualities on the part of the Confederate soldier. In the Gettysburg fight our men fought against great advantages held by the Union Army. They had numbers and position on us, and yet the old Confederate destroyed 75.7 per cent, of the 114th Pennsylvania Regiment and 73.8 of the 101st New York Regiment who fought from behind breastworks. This shows that position and numbers cut small figure with the Confederate soldier if he had just half a chance to shoot. In the Sharpsburg or Antietam fight in Maryland, the 20th Texas lost 83 per cent. of its number engaged, while the 12th Massachusetts lost but 76 per cent. At Antietam the Confederates fought against superior numbers and position and, I claim, we worsted McClellan in this battle. As a proof of this fact I present the following question: If General Lee was whipped in this fight and his army demoralized, as the historians of the North claim, why did not McClellan follow up his great victory and destroy General Lee before he could cross over the Potomac River?

The truth is just this: General Lee and his men in gray had so badly crippled the Union Army that they could not follow us, and those that did had cause to regret their temerity when Jackson waited for them at the river, at Sheperdstown Ford. These facts are all positive proof of my claims for the Confederate men in gray who were down in the mud.

In May, 1863, the Confederate Army was solely on the defensive. General Lee was confronted by Grant with a large and well-equipped army. From Spottsylvania to Cold Harbor it was a continual fight, in which General Grant and his army were always foiled.

The campaign begun by General Grant in the beginning of May, when he attacked Lee in the Wilderness, was made with an army of 118,000 men of all arms, according to the official statistics, while Lee's was given at 61,000, odds of very nearly two to one. When the campaign closed with the battle of Cold Harbor on June 1, Grant's losses were given as follows:

	Killed	Wounded
The Wilderness	2,246	12,037
Spottsylvania	2,725	13,416
North Anna	591	2,734
Cold Harbor	1,844	9,077
Sheridan's First Raid	64	337
Sheridan's Second Raid	150	741
Total	7,620	38,342

To these must be added the prisoners, making a grand total lost by Grant in that May campaign of 54,929, or nearly as many men as Lee's whole force and fully as many as he had for duty.

I read in some Report but a short time ago this fact, that there was less impacting of Confederate guns than there were of Union guns. The Confederate guns showed but 5 per cent., the Union guns over 30 per cent. What is meant by impacting is putting more than one charge into a gun. Now this is another claim for the Confederate soldiers' intelligence in the use of the gun at least.

The Surgeon-General's Report shows some interesting facts. There were killed and died of wounds during the war ('61-'65) 110,674 Union soldiers. The Confederate States' Surgeon-General's Report shows there were killed and died of wounds during 1861-'65, 67,000 Confederate soldiers. The number of Federal soldiers killed dead on the field was 74,524; Confederates killed dead on the field 53,773. So here, you see, we killed 20,751 more Union soldiers than our own loss. It is said, but I have not investigated its accuracy, that one out of every three men enlisted in the Confederate Army was killed or wounded. If these figures are compared with the death-rates in the great battles of the world, we are amazed at the death-rate of 1861-'65.

In the Russian war the loss was but 2.3 per cent. in each 100 men engaged; in the great Austrian war it was 2.6 per cent. in each 100 and in the Franco-Prussian war it was 3 per cent. in each 100. In the war of 1861-'65, the Federal loss was 4.7 per cent., while the Confederate loss was 9.5 per cent. in each 100 men engaged.

This last percentage is the largest death-rate recorded in history and presents another proof of the fighting qualities of the Confederate soldier. When we consider the arms he had until he captured better guns from the enemy we are lost in astonishment at the terrible execution and destruction the Confederate soldier did with his old flintlock gun. Yet here are the figures standing boldly out in confirmation of the claim that the Confederate soldier was intelligent, courageous and destructive.

The man in gray, who marched and toted the

gun, was a born fighter, whether he came from the schoolroom, the workshop or the field, and here are proofs of this. In the ranks of the Confederate Army there were 2,000 college professors and graduates, 400 of whom filled soldiers' graves. In the Union Army there were 1,040, of whom 155 filled soldiers' graves.

I do not believe we could build a monument too high or too costly to commemorate the valor and fidelity of the man in gray; the man behind the gun; the man who for principle alone faced death, hunger and cold, marched in the mud, braved death in all its hideous forms and was faithful unto the end for the cause of justice and right. I say build him a monument as high and as broad as the mountains; build him a monument that will be proof against the storms of time; let it be the record for the countless millions who shall follow us, that they may read the history of the men in gray who tramped in the mud and carried the gun.

Let it be the nation's tribute to the private soldier that the generations that come after us, in the flight of time, cannot say the South forgot her heroes. When this debt is paid the private Confederate soldier, living and dead, the man whose old gray jacket was the insignia of his nobility, a debt of honor long overdue, will be cancelled by the people of the South.

I want to present a few figures taken from the Report of the United States Commissary of Prisoners of War (General Ludlow Hoffman, 1861-'65) which is the most complete refutation of the slander that the Confederate authorities treated inhumanely their prisoners of war. These charges of cruelty are made in the press and pulpits of the North even at this late day. During the four years of the war the South held in her military prisons 270,000 Federal prisoners of war captured in the different battles. The United States had in her military prisons in the North 222,000 Confederate prisoners of war. So, by the figures of the United States Government, the South held 50,000 more prisoners of war in her prisons than the United States had Confederate prisoners of war in their prisons, and the Report of the United States Commissary of Prisoners of War shows that out of each one hundred Confederate prisoners held in Yankee prisons, twelve died, while out of each one hundred Yankee prisoners of war held in Southern prisons and camps, but eight died. Do not lose sight of this fact – it is very important to this statement. These figures are taken from the Report of the United States Commissary of Prisoners of War and not from the Confederate Report on the subject. Also bear in mind the South held 50,000 more prisoners of war than the United States and 48,000 more Confederate prisoners of war died in Yankee prisons than there were Federal prisoners of war died in Southern prisons. And yet we hear men, claiming intelligence in the North, crying out about Andersonville, the torture-house.

The United States Government had an abundance of rations, medicines, clothing and all else necessary to care for her prisoners of war to make them comfortable and keep them in health, while on the other hand the South had none of these things. The Confederate surgeons with the army were always short of medicines. So were our people. We had no clothing to give to our soldiers or prisoners, and often we had hardly rations to feed our armies. Our hospitals were always in need of the necessaries – let alone the comforts – and, notwithstanding all these drawbacks and insufficient supplies, 48,000 more prisoners of war died in Yankee prisons than Federal prisoners of war died in the prisons of the South.

The people who make the charges of cruelty to prisoners of war by the Confederate authorities are either unable to read or are wilful liars and slanderers.

Now, just a few more figures upon the relative strength of the Union and Confederate Armies, and I am done with figures.

Seven Days Fighting About Richmond

The Federal Army had 108,000
The Confederate Army had 80,726
____
Federal excess 27,274

Second Manassas

Federal Army 74,578
Confederate Army 49,770
____
Federal excess 24,808

Sharpsburg or Antietam

Federal Army 87,164
Confederate Army 35,225
____
Federal excess 51,939

Fredericksburg

Federal Army 100,000
Confederate Army 78,228
____
Federal excess 21,772

In this last battle General Lee used but 30,000 of his troops and beat General Burnside's army of 100,000. This is from the sworn testimony taken before the United States Committee of Congress on the Conduct of the War. General Burnside was the witness and knew what he was telling the Committee.

Chancellorsville

Federal Army 132,000
Confederate Army 57,000
____
Federal excess 75,000

Gettysburg

Federal Army 105,000
Confederate Army 62,000
____
Federal excess 43,800

General Grant's report shows more men in excess than General Lee had in his whole army on

February 28, 1865, when he fell back from Richmond to Petersburg. General Lee's whole force was 39,878 men. On March 1, 1865, his force, with nothing to eat and short of ammunition, was 33,000 men, while the report of General Grant's adjutant-general shows that Grant's army with plenty to eat, all the ammunition they needed and plenty of clothing, was 162,000 men – just 129,000 more than General Lee had, all told.

These figures, comrades, show the reason very clearly why you were compelled to lay down your arms on that April morn fifty years ago. You were not beaten; you were not whipped; nor were you unwilling to continue the unequal struggle. None of these causes made you lay down your arms. You were outnumbered; you were worn out from starvation and not by General Grant's army. Our beloved commander, Robert E. Lee, saw the useless sacrifice of life in continuing the hopeless struggle against a well-armed and well-fed army of double your numbers and recruited from all quarters of the globe. To that army the loss of men meant nothing; to us, one man's loss counted much.

The Men and Women of the South

In surrender the Confederate soldier lost none of his glory. He made a record nothing can dim. He snatched from the humility of his surrender to the greatly superior numbers of the foe the recognition of the world for his fidelity to the cause of right. From that field of Appomattox every Confederate soldier carried the love and respect of Robert E. Lee and the gratitude of the South and her people. And I do believe there was a prayer of thanks to heaven from more than one "Yank" that the war was done and he had escaped the deadly fire of your old flint-lock gun. When the end came the Confederate man of the ranks did not sit down and look in idleness upon the wreck and ruin of the war. No; he took up the burden as he found it. He brought his intelligence and courage to his assistance and began the work of rebuilding upon the ruins left him. He had no capital but his intelligence and courage. It was not long before he convinced the world that he could build as well as fight; and at no place in the South is the intelligence of the Confederate soldier more clearly shown than right here in this battle-scarred city of Winchester, made famous the world over by the immortal "Stonewall" Jackson and his men.

If you will take the trouble to investigate you will find I have not put an extravagant estimate upon the intelligence, courage and energy of the man in gray who was down in the mud. He has won rank in the professions; he has made his mark in the world of finance; he has acquired a place in the mercantile world. In the world of letters you find him and you can always discern his intelligence and pluck, hide it as he may. The Confederate soldier stands proudly before the world today commanding its respect for his adherence to the story of the past. He cannot forget the past, nor can he forget the moral support given to our cause in those days of blood by our noble women: I claim, always, for the peerless women of 1861-'65 a share in our glory of the past, and I do believe the women of that day were a potent factor in the cause. Their moral support and work for our army had much to do with our holding out as long as we did. Their love was essential to our endurance and victories. Without the love, fidelity and fortitude of our grand women I do believe the struggle would have ended before it did. Those women of 1861-'65 were truly the ministering angels of the Confederate soldier. Their share in our glory cannot be questioned. When we were hungry they fed us, when sick they nursed us back to health, when wounded they bathed our wounds with a tear, when stricken upon the battlefield, they were the angel messengers bearing our loved ones far away for the last good-bye. Their story is part and parcel of our story. Their deeds are engraved deeply upon the hearts of the men who love the past. We bowed, in those days, in admiration of those golden locks; today we doff our caps in veneration to the "silver threads among the gold."

We can never forget the memories of the past nor the work of the noble women whose names are written upon the scroll of fame. Theirs is a grand old story to tell over and over again. It is a story of love, devotion and fortitude. It is part of the story of the cause we loved and lost.

From the birth of the Confederacy to its death on Appomattox field our peerless women gave the world an example of love and devotion that was not surpassed by the women of Sparta or Rome. When the true history of the great conflict is written our women of '61-'65 must have their page with ours. It was written long ago in the blood of our bravest men, and in the tears of our noblest women. The history of the South cannot be written nor the story truthfully told if our women of that day have no place in it. As the days go by these noble women are passing away. We thank God for His goodness in giving us in our days of trial such women. There are few of that noble band left – many have passed over the river and are now residents of God's Eternal City of Love. They loved us in life – they love us still – and I do believe they plead in prayer for us before God's mercy seat.

So let us try and live, while on this march through life, that, when the order is given us to halt beyond the picket line of life, we may hear, coming through the pearly gates, the angel voices of these dear women of the Confederacy, saying: "Weary, foot-sore, old Confederate soldier, thou hast kept the faith unto the end; God, our Father, bids you welcome into rest."

I would not forget the Daughters of the South today who have taken the work of their sainted mothers and friends. God bless you in all your work and aid you always, and give you always the loyalty, devotion and strength your mothers gave to the cause we loved and lost in the days when the land was deluged with the blood of loved ones, defending our homes, the Constitution and the law.

Statistics of the Opposing Armies

The following being a signed article and knowing Mr. Elder, I use it as matter of interest to the student of history and the public.

Birmingham, Ala., June 11, 1908.

Editor of the *Birmingham News*,

Sir – Believing that some of the veterans visiting your magnificent city, as well as other readers of your paper, would be interested in the statistics of the United States and Confederate armies of 1861-1865, I give below the official and total enlistment in each army, foreign as well as native born, which we divide into four armies as follows:

Germany furnished	176,500
Ireland	14,420
England	45,500
Other countries	253,500
New York State	448,850
Pennsylvania	337,936
Total	489,920
Illinois	259,092
Indiana	196,336
Ohio	313,108
Total	768,536
Slave and border States	454,416
New England States	363,161
Total	817,577

Grand Total 2,878,304

It will be seen from the above enlistments that the United States had four armies equal to or superior in numbers to the Confederate army.

The grand total of these four armies was 2,878,304. The total enlistment of the Confederate States 600,000, making an excess in the United States army of 2,278,304.

The question which confronts us is, how did these 600,000 men composing the Confederate army wear themselves out whipping this immense army of 2,878,304, composed of the best equipped and fed army the world ever saw?

Will some of my old comrades solve the problem for me?

Very respectfully.

J.H. Elder, of Atlanta, Ga.

PART III
The South's Peerless Women

CHAPTER EIGHT

☆ ☆ ☆ ☆

Ministering Angels of the Confederate Soldier

At the urgent request of dear old comrades of the past, whose love and good will I cherish, this tribute to the women of the South, past and present, is printed in this book. It is only the author's love and respect for our peerless women of the United Daughters of the Confederacy. It is fact briefly stated of the work of the Southland. In the days when the fanatics of the North attempted to destroy the political liberties of the South, the women of the Confederacy were the ministering angels of the Confederate soldier, as their daughters today are the angels of mercy and charity, working for and caring for the Veterans of 1861-'65. The friends who urge that this paper shall be printed say it is for the purpose of voicing the love and loyalty of all true Confederate soldiers, who honestly wore the gray, and that the publication may induce our young people of today to look up and investigate the part their mothers took in the war of 1861-'65.

Our women of the South were the inspiration of the Confederate soldier. On the battlefield, in camp, on the march, their love, loyalty and devotion taught the world a lesson of fidelity worth the learning. It was written on the scroll of fame – a glorious story that will never be effaced by Time's relentless hand. None will deny that the women of the South of 1861-'65 must have their page in Confederate history, and we do hold that if they do not have their page, the history cannot be a complete nor correct one of the days when the Southland made history of which no man who wore the gray need be ashamed.

Our children of the South should certainly be taught in our schools and in their homes the true story of 1861-'65, and the part their mothers took in the struggle of Might against Right, that in all places and at all times they may be able to refute the slanders of the Northern historians, whose histories were forced on our schools by the Carpet Baggers that were foisted upon us after the war.

The brightest gems of a nation's coronet are the ashes of its heroic dead, and this I grant is true, but there is another priceless gem in the Southland's coronet, and this gem is the peerless women of the Southland – the noble mothers, the moral support of all nations, who teach their children the principles of liberty, justice, and obedience to law. These are the principles that make nations great, these the principles that make the great soldiers, statesmen, and heroes of all nations. It was these principles that gave the Southland in her hour of need Jefferson

Davis, Robert E. Lee, "Stonewall" Jackson, and the other noble leaders of the Confederacy.

No people on earth can claim greater statesmen, grander soldiers, nor braver women than the South. The Colonial mothers in 1776 made the Colonial soldier what he was – invincible. The women of the South in the days of our peril made the Confederate soldier the ideal soldier of the world. No one can deny that the women of the South in 1861-'65 were a potent factor in our holding out in the unequal struggle as long as we did. In our darkest days these peerless mothers bid us look up to God. They trusted; they prayed for us; they worked for us; they stood sponsor for the Infant Confederacy when it was baptized in the best blood of the South; they mourned with us at the grave of the Republic and buried liberty on Appomattox field.

The women of the Confederacy from 1861-'65 suffered as no other women on earth were ever called upon to suffer. At times it was even a question of food with which to feed their children. The people on the plantations had their property devastated, their homes robbed and burned by the Yankee soldiers, while they, themselves, were subjected to insult by the brutal invader, who ignored all rules of civilized warfare and humanity. But all this persecution could not shake their faith, nor lessen the love they held for the cause of their beloved South. "No braver dames had Sparta, no nobler matrons Rome," than the South had in her peerless daughters, when the mourning crepe hung from every door, when the invader's torch wrought ruin of our homes, and when hearts were pierced by sorrow's sword – and this was true of all the women of the South. I care not if she came from the lowly cot on the hillside, or from the gilded halls of wealth in the vale, she was a heroine, a daughter of the South, and she was peerless in her devotion.

Some of these grand women had given their all to the cause they loved. Hear the words of the Spartan mother of the South. She had given her two older boys to the cause, but hear her words, as she buckled on the sword of her only boy, "My son, your country needs your services. Go! Come back to me in honor, or come back on your shield." And this was that noble mother's consecration upon her country's altar in Liberty's holy name, and she was only one of Southern mothers.

On the battlefields, when the carnage was done, you found these noble women ministering to the wounded, taking the last message from the dying soldier to his loved ones far away. You found them in our hospitals, and from wherever came the cry of distress you found these ministering angels of the South, doing their part without ostentation, without murmur. They shared our perils; they must share our praise for their love and devotion to the Confederate soldier. Give them all this right.

An English gentleman once gave a commission to a celebrated artist for a canvas. He said, "Paint for me a picture that will appeal to the heart, and not to the eye alone." The artist was in a quandary what he should paint. He appealed to an old Crimean soldier for a subject, and the soldier took from his pocket an old pen picture of Florence Nightingale kneeling at the cotside of a dying soldier, taking his farewell message for his loved ones in an English home. And from that crude sketch he painted a picture that has appealed to the heart of the world in his beautiful canvas "Consolation," and one that has brought more silent prayers from the hearts of men and women than any other painting ever has.

Had this artist asked any loved Confederate soldier for a subject, he would have simply handed him a photograph of any one of the sainted women of 1861-'65, told him the story of that woman in the war, her love, devotion, fidelity, and courage, and what a canvas the artist could have given the world. England had one Florence Nightingale – God bless her noble soul – but the South had thousands of women as devoted and true. When we who wore the gray now look back on those days of blood, and recall the peerless women, there comes from way down deep in our hearts that beautiful prayer, "O God, be with us still, lest we forget, lest we forget the ministering angels of the Southland, who prayed for us, who worked for us." We owe a debt to the women of the war days, and those of today, but we owe to God a greater debt – that He gave us such women in the days of our need.

And may I repeat that our grand women of the war days were the ministering angels of the soldiers in Gray. You found them at the cotside, in the hospitals, nursing back to life the sick and wounded, and I do know that oftimes in their charity their help was extended to the Federal soldiers that the fate of the battle had left in our hands. And yet, you can find in some of the Northern histories of today the slander that our daughters of the South refused aid to the stricken Union soldiers in our hospitals. Perish the tongue that uttered such slander; wither the hand that wrote such vile falsehoods of the peerless women of the South.

Ingenuity and Industry of the Southern Women

When the crisis came, our women met it; economy took the place of plenty; luxuries were for the hospitals only. The homespun dress took the place of fine linen; the sick and wounded was their care, and without one selfish thought they divided with the sick and needy their scanty hoard of food. In truth they were ministering angels of the Confederate soldier. They were the inspiration of the Confederacy. Their deeds of love and charity are deeply engraved upon the hearts of all men who wore the Gray. When the story of the Confederacy is truthfully told, when the part our women took in the war is read, the world will bow their heads in admiration and veneration for the women of the Southland, where honor is held dearer than life and womanhood peerless.

When war's grim harvest was done, these women of the South did not halt in their works of mercy, love and charity, ground down as they were by the rule of the Carpet Bagger from the North, whose hate and malice was exceeded only by his thieving desires. The noble women organized themselves into bands and began collecting the remains of our heroic dead, placing them in cemeteries, marking each sacred grave, and the same gentle hands that soothed the soldiers' fevered brows, and bound up their wounds, kept green the sod above their heroic graves. But was this all these women did? No. They took upon themselves the care and education of the Confederate soldiers' orphan children; they took upon themselves the care and support of the needy Confederate veteran who had given his all for the cause of the Southern Cross in the struggle for Justice and Right.

Daughters of the Confederacy of today, when your mothers were called to rest, in God's City of Rest, they gave into your hands, they bequeathed to you a sacred trust that you should take up this work where they left off, that you should go on building monuments, caring for the orphans and needy old veterans who wore the gray, and that you should keep green the sod above the graves of our sacred dead, and keep alive the grand old story, and traditions of your sainted mothers. Have you kept this trust? Let the Confederate veteran answer this question for you! And like the roar of the mighty ocean, from the mountain tops of old Virginia, from the Gulf Stream of the farthest South comes back the answer, "Yes, she has kept the trust, proved herself worthy the daughter of a peerless mother." And I say that your organization of the United Daughters of the Confederacy of today has done more to perpetuate the grand old story of the past than any other organization of the South.

Who can say, who dare say that our cause was a Lost Cause? Who can say the Confederate soldier will be forgotten while these Daughters of the Confederacy are erecting monuments, or placing tablets of brass and bronze at some spot in the South to perpetuate the valor and glory of the man who wore the gray. When we have the evidence of all his work before us, tell me how it can be possible that the grand old story of the past will be a forgotten, untold story? When the Bugle of Time shall sound taps for all the men who wore the gray, these worthy daughters of royal mothers will still tell the story of the Confederacy to posterity, and the world will always hear the story of Jefferson Davis, the statesman; Robert E. Lee, the immortal; "Stonewall" Jackson, the invincible; Ashby, the cavalier; Forrest, the unconquered; Morgan, the dauntless; Pettigrew, the grand; Stewart, the peerless, and the other heroic souls who carried the flag and led the Confederate soldier to victory on many bloody fields of battle. The mothers of today will tell to the lisping babe the story of the man in gray, and it will live forever.

Tell to the world whatever you will, men of the South, of the women of the war and today. I do not care how extravagant it may sound to other ears, the man who wore the gray knows the story is true. He knows the women of 1861-'65, in the South, fairly won our adoration and love, and all we can say of them is that, as the Daughters of today, by their fidelity, loyalty, and charity they have won our love and loyalty to them.

We have often thought of an emblem for the United Daughters organization, and I found in the Floral Kingdom (that wonderful exhibition of God's most exquisite handiwork, where we are lost in adoration for His great love for the human race presented to us in things beautiful) a fitting emblem for the Daughters of the Confederacy of today in that matchless combination of beauty and fragrance – the Night Blooming Cereus, which generously contributes its odors to the world's store of fragrance, but modestly conceals its beauty behind the veil of night. And this is the emblem of the daughters of the South, of the past and of today. They perform their works of love and charity without ostentation or show, claiming no reward, asking no pay, save that which comes to the heart of a duty well done.

The Charge of the United Daughters

The daughters of the South today are following closely in the footsteps of their peerless mothers, in charity, loyalty, and love. Daughters of the Confederacy, the story of the past is yours to tell. Tell it over and over again. It will gladden the heart of the old Confederate veteran. It will take him back to the days when his soul was tried by the sword, and his manhood by shot and shell. I wish that I could paint for you and the world the grand old story of the noblest womanhood of the world. In the Book of Life, in the indelible ink of God's love, the story of your sainted mothers of the war days is written. It can never fade; it will never dim. If the curtain of the past that hides from this generation the days of the war could be pushed back, then indeed would they see the true pictures of their ancestors, and you could then fully understand why the Confederate soldier loves the woman of the Southland, of the past and present.

The picture I have tried to paint for you, Daughters of today, of our women of 1861-'65 was painted long ago. It was painted when the sword flashed death to the flower of the Southland. It was painted by the glare of the invader's torch that destroyed our homes. It is the picture of consecration and love. It is the story of what your mothers endured. It cheered the Confederate soldier on to deeds of valor that startled the world. Daughters of today, your mothers were indeed the inspiration of the Confederate soldier. It was her sublime courage and hope that drove despair from our hearts and bid the dove of hope spread his white wings about us. When the heart of the South was bowed in grief, when hope had fled, we learned to love and venerate our noble women, and we knew we possessed the peerless womanhood of the world. They prayed for us and we bow now in love and veneration for the consecration they made for us as we felt the love and charity for the Confederate soldier today. It comes to us like the benediction after the prayer.

Sons and Daughters of the South, you can only know from traditions handed down to you the grandeur of your mothers of the war days. You will hand the story down to your children. It is a grand old story; guard it well; forget it never! This grand old story of our women brings back to the Confederate veteran's heart sweet memories in his old age. He lives again the days of the past. These memories fill his old heart with joy. They cling about him like the vines of the Orient to the oak, and from his old heart comes the prayer, "God bless and keep our noble women of the Southland, our ministering angels, in charity and love."

It is sweet to the old veteran in gray to live in retrospection those terrible days of the past. We can now better appreciate the joys and forget the pains. In the dreamland of retrospection the women of the war days are with us, and we doff our caps in admiration of their golden curls. We awake from the dream to the stern reality that Time has set his frosty hand upon their heads, and we bow in veneration to the silver that has replaced the gold.

We are all drifting on the river of time in frail barques. We are sailing on to the ocean of eternity, and yet we revel in the memories of those days, when we donned the suit of gray and marched away to battle for our homes and loved ones. We all hoped to return in triumph to lay at the feet of our dear ones laurels honestly won. We took no care of the morrow. In the enthusiasm of youth we forgot the dangers of war; we heard not the rustle of the wings of death; we heard not the voice of destruction, and its attendant death. Some who marched away returned; some fell in the fray. They sleep the sleep of the brave and true, and their graves are marked and kept green by the loving hands of the daughters of today, and these ministering angels of today are keeping the sacred trust given them by their mothers, and are teaching the world today a lesson of fidelity, loyalty and love.

The mothers of the war days are, like ourselves, passing away. Their ranks, like our own, grow less each day. But they have left to us who wore the gray worthy daughters, who will tell the grand old story of their mothers, and will live while time lasts. It is said a good story can be ruined by too much telling. This may be true of a large majority of stories and causes, but it is not true of the story of the Confederacy, and its peerless women, who stood with us in the great struggle of the South for liberty, justice, and law.

The grand women of the South of today have all the force of character of their mothers. They have the loyalty, fidelity and love that the world admires. Daughters of the United Daughters of the Confederacy, your mothers wrote their story on the scroll of fame for you in the days of war. It is your story. Tell it whenever you choose and wherever you may. You will always have men who love loyalty and fidelity and courage to listen with eager ears Your story is the story of the South in her days of peril, and the prosperity of today in the South shows her sons could fight and could build upon the ruins wrought by war.

There are but a few of the grand women of the war days left. They have crossed over the river into the land of God. They are residents of His eternal city of love, and I do believe they plead daily before Mercy's throne for us, so I say to every man who wore the gray, "Let us try and live so that when we are called to join our comrades now at rest, when we reach the City of Golden Gates we may hear the voices of our sainted women saying, 'Weary, footsore, old Confederate Veteran, thou has kept the faith unto the end. God, our Father, bids us welcome you into rest.'"

Daughters of the Confederacy, when you are called to join your mothers in that better world, the land of God's love, I pray your crowns may be the brightest, studded with the gems of God's love, and each crown bear the proud inscription "Daughters of the Confederacy, ministering angels of the South's veteran sons."

And may I say to you in closing, if the Confederate veteran had a thousand lives, he would live them for you; if he had a thousand hearts, he would give them all to you!

Letter from Mrs. Jefferson Davis

This letter was sent to Major Murray in reply to a manuscript submitted to Mrs. Davis.

123 West 44th Street, New York.

My Dear Major Murray: –

I have not offered you thanks because insensible to your stirring address or your kindness in affording me the perusal of it, but I have an immense correspondence, and am very old and quite feeble. Shortly after your letter reached me I was stricken by a severe illness from which I have not yet recovered, and so have not made grateful acknowledgment for the noble address, which my dear old friend Colonel Park so kindly asked you to send me.

The "policy of silence," as to my husband's eminent and devoted service and glad sacrifice for the Confederacy, has been pursued until it has seemed to me that those to whom his whole heart was given, had changed towards him. Your eloquent outpouring of enthusiastic esteem and confidence in him has put fresh heart in me, and I wish he could have lived to read it. Gratefully and cordially.

Your friend,
Varina Jefferson Davis.

February 5, 1903.

Made in the USA
Monee, IL
07 July 2026

56551692R00085